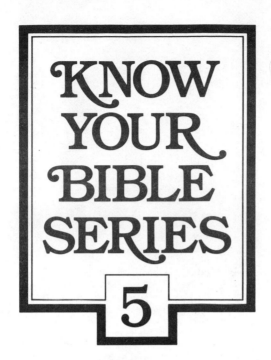

# KNOW YOUR BIBLE SERIES

## 5

**GENESIS
EXODUS
LEVITICUS
NUMBERS
DEUTERONOMY**

## ROY L. SMITH

ABINGDON PRESS
NASHVILLE

Genesis, Exodus, Leviticus, Numbers, Deuteronomy

No. 209161

Printed in U.S.A.

# INTRODUCTION

To the average readers of the Bible the period of the Babylonian Exile probably has little significance. This is because we have small appreciation of the forces which played upon the life of the Jews during those fateful years. We do not know, for instance, that the bases of their religious faith were completely altered; we are unaware of the fact that an entirely new series of religious institutions came into existence among them. If we have given any thought to the matter at all, we are probably under the impression that those years constituted a spiritual vacuum in which nothing of importance happened. No kings were crowned, no wars were waged, no territory was won. Judged by events such as are usually chosen by historians as yardsticks of history, the Exile was little more than a succession of "lost years" between the collapse of the kingdom of Judah and the establishment of the Second Commonwealth.

The simple truth is, however, that the period between 597 B.C., when the first deportees were carried away to Babylonia, and about 400 B.C., when Ezra presided over the convocation which established the Book of the Law as the divinely inspired constitution of the Jews, is one of the most creative in all the annals of the Hebrew race. During those years the unique religious institutions which distinguish modern Judaism came into existence. The peculiar practices by which the Jew of today expresses his deepest spiritual longings all root back in the experience of the Exile.

Even more important, from our viewpoint, is the influence of the Exile on the development of the Sacred Scriptures. As we come to understand the processes which operated through those dark years, we discover that large sections of the Old Testament consist of writings which passed through thrilling adventures before they arrived at their present status as scripture.

Devout scholars, with profound learning at their backs, have given many years to the task of unearthing the facts involved in the production of our Bible in its modern form. They have stood reverently in the presence of its sacred pages and allowed them to speak in their own behalf. Instead of coming to the Book with a theory and compelling it to prove that theory, they have

3

approached it with an open mind and allowed it to offer its own evidence. On the basis of all the facts they were able to uncover, they have developed their interpretations.

They learned, for instance, that a small book of law was found in the Jerusalem Temple in 621 B.C., during the reign of the good King Josiah, and that it was proclaimed to be the sacred book of law—a written constitution—for the nation. This was, so far as any record in the Bible indicates, the first writing ever to be accorded the status of "scripture" by the Hebrews. Then they discovered that a great "Book of the Law" was officially proclaimed to be the divinely inspired governmental code of the nation about 400 B.C. Naturally they wanted to know what these books were and what they contained. This study is a report of the decisions they have reached.

ROY L. SMITH

# The First Jewish Bible

**1** **Do the Jews have a Bible?**

Most assuredly. As a matter of fact their Bible was the only Scriptures the Christians had for nearly two hundred years. The Bible of the Christians rest squarely on the Hebrew Scriptures just as the faith of the Christians roots back in the religion of the Hebrews.

**2** **Of what does the Jewish Bible consist?**

It consists of the Books contained in what is called the Old Testament in the Protestant Bible.

**3** **Are they the same as in our Protestant Old Testament?**

They differ in only two respects: (1) the order in which they appear, and (2) slight variations in the text.

**4** **What is their order in the Jewish Old Testament?**

| | | |
|---|---|---|
| Genesis | Ezekiel | Psalms |
| Exodus | Hosea | Proverbs |
| Leviticus | Joel | Job |
| Numbers | Amos | Song of Songs |
| Deuteronomy | Obadiah | Ruth |
| Joshua | Jonah | Lamentations |
| Judges | Micah | Ecclesiastes |
| I Samuel | Nahum | Esther |
| II Samuel | Habakkuk | Daniel |
| I Kings | Zephaniah | Ezra |
| II Kings | Haggai | Nehemiah |
| Isaiah | Zechariah | I Chronicles |
| Jeremiah | Malachi | II Chronicles |

**5** **What is the reason for this arrangement?**

The Jews of Jesus' day divided their scriptures into three major divisions. Just as modern Christians speak of the Old and New Testaments, so the Jews spoke of the "Law," the

"Prophets," and the "Writings." Furthermore, just as the two testaments were accorded the status of scripture at different times, so the three divisions of the Jewish Bible rose to the dignity of being called scripture at different times.

The first books to be so honored came to be known as the "Law" because they contained the rules by which the people chosen by God were expected to live. About two hundred years later a collection of the sermons of the great prophets came to be considered scripture and was called the "Prophets." For many years the Hebrew sacred books were known as "the Law and the Prophets," and Jesus referred to them by that name (Matthew 11:13; 22:40; Luke 16:16) even though in his day a third collection known as the "Writings" was associated with the first two divisions. This last collection was not officially designated as scripture, however, until the Council of Jamnia, which convened about A.D. 90. The Jewish Bible retains the original order, while in our Christian Bible the books have been slightly rearranged.

## 6 Which are the books of the Law?

The five books of the Law were originally no more than sections of what was known to the Jews from about 400 B.C. as the "Book of the Law." It was presented to the people of Jerusalem by Ezra the scribe as a single work. But, early writing materials being fragile, it was too long to go on one scroll of practical size and had to be copied in several "volumes." Soon five divisions became fixed, and on translation into Greek they were given the names by which we know them—Genesis, Exodus, Leviticus, Numbers, Deuteronomy.

The Jews divided their prophetical books into two groups, which they called the "Former Prophets" and the "Latter Prophets." The first group consisted of the six Old Testament books known to us as Joshua, Judges, First and Second Samuel, and First and Second Kings. The second group consisted of Isaiah, Jeremiah, Ezekiel, and the "Book of the Twelve." This latter book was one great one containing the sermons of Hosea, Joel, Amos, Obadiah, Jonah, Micah, Nahum, Habakkuk, Zephaniah, Haggai, Zechariah, and Malachi. Modern students usually speak of them as the "major prophets" and the "minor

6

prophets." These designations have been given them because of their bulk, rather than their importance, Isaiah, Jeremiah, and Ezekiel being long books and the twelve very much shorter ones. The Former Prophets have come to be known to Christian scholars as historical books and have been treated as such in this series of studies.

## 8  Why were they called prophetical books?

The Jews used the word "prophet" to designate someone who taught a great truth. The Former Prophets are writings which undertook to teach the nation that God would prosper Israel if it was loyal to him and would punish it if it was disloyal. This teaching purpose of the books gave them the name of prophetical books.

## 9  Which are the Writings?

The remaining thirteen books of the Old Testament—Psalms, Proverbs, Job, Song of Songs, Ruth, Lamentations, Ecclesiastes, Esther, Daniel, Ezra, Nehemiah, First and Second Chronicles. The scholars are generally agreed that the two books of Chronicles were originally combined in one, along with Nehemiah and Ezra. In some cases the Song of Songs, Ruth, Lamentations, Esther, and Ecclesiastes were combined in one collection and called the "Five Rolls."

## 10  What about the variations in the text?

(See Question No. 3.) If we read almost any chapter out of the Jewish Bible alongside the corresponding chapter in a Protestant Bible, we will be apt to notice occasional differences in words, phrases, or perhaps even whole sentences. In very few instances, however, will there be noted any real differences in meaning. Nevertheless these variations do call for an explanation.

## 11  What is that explanation?

The original authors of the books of the Old Testament wrote in Hebrew, for the most part, and their writings were read in that language for several centuries. The original copies penned by the authors themselves have all passed out of existence, but copies were made, and then copies of copies. It was inevitable that mistakes would be made in the process of copying, and some of these mistakes were perpetuated in the copies made from incorrect texts. As the scholars study these ancient manuscripts, they endeavor as best they can to determine what may have been the exact form of the original writing, and in such cases it is inevitable that there will be differences of opinion. When the English Christian translators produced the King James Version of the Bible in 1611, they used what they considered the best Hebrew text available, and their translation was accepted by English Protestant readers as being the standard text. When the Jewish scholars translated the Old Testament into English for the benefit of English-reading Jews, they used what they considered the best Hebrew text available to them; but as might be expected, their judgment of the best text differed slightly. Furthermore, even when they agreed on the text, they used English words with a slightly different meaning to express the ideas contained in the Hebrew. And their text was accepted by the Jews as their standard text.

## 12 Which is the correct translation?

That is purely a question of scholarly judgment. It often happens that a Hebrew word conveys more than one meaning and may be capable of several translations. It becomes then a question which must be settled by the translator, who gives the matter his most careful thought and finally adopts the English word which, in his opinion, most accurately expresses what he believes to have been the idea of the original author.

## 13 Do all modern Scriptures derive from the same originals?

They do. The Jewish, Catholic, and Protestant Old Testaments have all come down to us from the same Hebrew writings, which means that all three faiths have the largest part of their Bible in common. Whatever differences we find in the English versions they use can be explained by the differences in the translations they have accepted as being standard.

## 14 Is the Jewish Bible published in Hebrew?

There is now an accepted Hebrew text of the Old Testament

8

which is used by scholars of all faiths. It represents the most nearly accurate reproduction of the original it has been possible for modern scholarship to produce so far, but textual studies for improving it still continue. This text is used by Jewish scholars in their researches, but the average English-speaking Jew unversed in the niceties of the ancient Hebrew depends upon his standard English translation just as the average Christian reader depends upon the King James Version, or one of the Revised Versions, whichever happens to be his preference.

## 15 What is the standard Jewish version?

It is a translation of the Hebrew Old Testament which has been authorized and approved by the Association of American Rabbis (for American readers) and which is the product of the finest scholarship available among the Jews. Like Christian translators, the Jewish scholars have consulted all the ancient manuscripts, as well as other versions, in their effort to discover the exact form of the original writings.

## 16 What about the ancient manuscripts and other versions?

Modern scholars, both Christian and Jewish, have access to a considerable number of old Hebrew manuscripts, some of which contain portions of the Old Testament, and others of which contain large sections or even the entire Old Testament. Then there are at least four versions which have come down to us by different lines of descent, each of which has considerable value for the light it throws on difficult passages. They are: (1) the Septuagint and other early Greek versions, (2) the Syriac version, (3) the Latin Vulgate, and (4) the Samaritan Pentateuch.

## 17 Are the manuscripts really valuable?

They are, probably, the most valuable single source we have for studying the ancient text. Of the many hundreds in existence some have little value and others are of great importance. This matter was investigated in some detail in Study No. 1 of this series, but it is necessary at this time to add some information concerning the development of Hebrew writing, for some Old Testament problems of very great interest revolve about this matter.

## 18   What is the story of the development of Hebrew writing?

The Hebrew alphabet in use among the ancients consisted of twenty-two consonants. For many years no vowel signs of any kind were used, and no spaces were inserted between words. As long as the Hebrew language was used in everyday speech this was a satisfactory arrangement, for the pronunciations were all well known. But by the time of the third century A.D., when Hebrew was spoken only by scholars, a feeling began to develop that the alphabet was inadequate, and certain consonants began to be used to express unchangeably long vowels. By the middle of the sixth century Hebrew, as a spoken language, was dying out even among the scholars, and there was a serious danger that the proper pronunciations would be lost. About the beginning of the seventh century a guild of Jewish scribes, known as Massoretes (Traditionists), introduced a system of points to accompany the consonants and indicate the vowel sounds as traditionally pronounced.

Long before the Massoretes introduced their innovation the text of the Hebrew Scriptures had come to be regarded as absolutely sacred by the Jews. The Massoretes were scrupulously careful, then, to make no changes in the text. In some cases they even copied meaningless signs which had crept by accident into the text—marks perhaps inscribed by some reader many years before for his private guidance. But by introducing the vowel signs they did actually become interpreters of the text in some instances.

Suppose we came upon the English constants BLL and were asked to supply the necessary vowel to make the proper word for completing a sentence. We might suggest any one of the five vowels and get an entirely different word in each case. To use BALL, BELL, BILL, BOLL, or BULL would give an altogether different meaning to each of the five sentences. From this simple illustration it is easy to see how the Massoretes, by inventing the system of vowel points, actually gave us an interpretation of the consonated text, for *they supplied all the vowels*. In this way, and because of the belief of the Jews in an absolutely sacred text, they gave us a "standard" Hebrew Old Testament.

## 19 Is the Massoretic text accepted as standard today?

It is the standard text used by both Jewish and Christian scholars. They regard it with even more respect since the discovery in 1947 of the Dead Sea scrolls, which contain copies of Isaiah and part of Habakkuk believed to date from the first century B.C. Other than these the oldest Hebrew manuscript we have of any considerable section of the Old Testament goes back only to A.D. 916, and the oldest complete text only to the eleventh century. Yet in spite of a thousand years of copyings there are only insignificant differences between the Dead Sea and Massoretic texts. Nevertheless the scholars recognize the likelihood of errors and not only study all available manuscripts of the Hebrew text but also consult the early versions, especially the Septuagint, in order to find the correct readings.

## 20 What was the Septuagint?

Somewhere around 250 B.C. the Book of the Law was translated into Greek by a group of Jewish scholars at Alexandria. Little is known about either the circumstances or the persons who did the work, but the translation came to be called the Septuagint because of a tradition that it was made by seventy scholars. As other books were accepted as scripture they were also translated and added to the Septuagint. This translation was the standard Greek version in Jesus' day, and became the Bible of the early Christians, most of whom spoke Greek and did not know Hebrew. Most of the quotations from the Old Testament that appear in the New Testament were taken from the Septuagint rather than directly from the Hebrew—which explains why the wording is often different (for example, compare Luke 4:18-19 with Isaiah 61:1-2). Use by the Christians had the effect of discrediting the Septuagint among the Jews and led to other Greek translations to take its place. Early in the second century a convert to Judaism named Aquila made a translation so literal that Greek readers could scarcely understand it. Later in the same century Symmachus the Ebionite made a much better translation, and about the same time a famous scholar named Theodotion revised the Septuagint to fit Jewish standards. Many Christian manuscripts of the Septuagint are available, but only fragments of the other Greek versions have survived.

# 21 What was the Syriac version?

The Syriac language, a dialect somewhat akin to Hebrew, was spoken throughout Syria and Mesopotamia outside of Palestine until sometime after the Arab conquest in the seventh century A.D. At some time not now known, between the second and fifth centuries, some Syrian Christians translated the Old Testament into Syriac. Of a few of the books it was a literal translation, of others a free translation, and of the rest it was little more than a paraphrase; but it has proved of value when studied alongside the other texts.

# 22 What was the Latin Vulgate?

By A.D. 405 the western half of the Christian Church was composed of persons who used Latin in their daily conversations. With the Old Testament available in the Septuagint version, and the New Testament written originally in Greek—some scholars believe some portions may have been composed in Aramaic, a Semitic dialect akin to Hebrew, and translated into Greek by a later hand—the entire Bible was to be had in that language. But the masses had outlived the Greek as they had earlier outlived the Hebrew. Individuals here and there had undertaken to translate portions of the Scriptures into Latin, and there were actually a few "Old Latin" translations, but they were both inaccurate and usually incomplete. Toward the close of the fourth century the need of an authoritative translation of the Scriptures became evident; and Jerome, the leading Christian scholar of the day, was commissioned by the leaders of the Church to undertake the task. He completed his work, and the Bible was issued in its new Latin version in A.D. 405, becoming the standard translation and remaining so for many years. One of the unique features of Jerome's work lay in the fact that in addition to consulting the Septuagint and other Greek versions he actually made a careful study of such Hebrew manuscripts as were available to him and which seemed to him to have real value.

# 23 What was the Samaritan Pentateuch?

It was a version of the Book of the Law preserved by the Samaritans from the time of Ezra (about 400 B.C.). It varies from the standard Jewish and Christian versions of the Pentateuch in about six thousand items, of which perhaps as many as a thousand have some significance.

## 24 What caused these differences?

A few are a result of a deliberate effort on the part of the Samaritans to make their scripture support their position in their dispute with the Jews. Others are, of course, the inevitable mistakes that occur in copying. The standards of scholarship among the Samaritans have never been so high as among the Jews, with the result that their scribes were much less expert. The effect is very noticeable in their copies of the Scriptures, which are very imperfect.

## 25 Who were the Samaritans?

When the Assyrians deported the Israelites to the number of 27,290 in the year 721 B.C. and thus brought the kingdom of Israel to an inglorious end, they filled the country with deportees from other subjugated lands (II Kings 17:24). Within a few years the population became a mongrel sort with a culture that was an amalgam of elements from all the East. Assyria did not deport all the Israelites, only the upper classes. Many thousands were left in the rural areas, and these continued to worship according to a form of Yahweh faith. The conglomerate population came to be known as Samaritans from the name of the ancient capital, Samaria. When the exiles returned from Babylonian captivity, a sharp rivalry was not long in developing.

## 26 What was the cause of this conflict?

The first Jews returning from Babylonia in 536 B.C. began rehabilitating the land and rebuilding the Jerusalem Temple. But they were very few, very poor, and their discouragements multiplied. It was not long until they lost heart and accepted conditions as they found them; and news of this sorry state of affairs filtering back to Babylon resulted in a new expedition under the leadership of a patriotic layman named Nehemiah (about 445 B.C.), the purpose of which was to rebuild the Temple and purge the nation of its alien elements. Shortly after Nehemiah's arrival in Jerusalem, some Samaritans appealed for the chance to assist in the enterprise and were refused. They were, in a sense, coreligionists, for they also worshiped Yahweh. They were also kindred of a sort, and there is some reason to believe their gesture was sincere, though the Biblical records report it otherwise. One of the major purposes of Nehemiah's enterprise was to purge the Jewish community of all alien influences, that it might be acceptable to Yahweh. In accordance with that purpose Nehemiah's program called for a strict supervision of all marriages in order that no alien blood might pollute the nation's heritage. Strict orders were issued against all alliances with non-Hebrews.

When the Babylonian exiles had returned in 536 B.C., they had re-established the high priesthood in Jerusalem; and Nehemiah discovered to his horror that a grandson of the high priest was married to a Samaritan woman, the daughter of Sanballat, the Samaritan governor. It was entirely possible that someday the young man might become high priest himself, and it was unthinkable that the head of the Jewish theocracy should be married to an alien woman. To Nehemiah this was revolting in the extreme, and he had but one remedy—he cast the young man out of the Jewish community (Nehemiah 13:23-28). This was an affront the Samaritans could not overlook. The honor of the governor himself was involved. Josephus tells us that the young man was welcomed into the Samaritan community and made the high priest of the new Samaritan cult. A temple was built for him on Mount Gerizim, the Book of the Law was altered to suit Samaritan purposes, and a rival religion was instituted. From this time on the two religions persisted side by side, bitter rivals, each claiming to be the true faith of Yahweh. The Samaritans never accepted either the Prophets or the Writings as scripture, and their Bible continues to this day as a version of the Pentateuch.

## 27 How do all these versions help the scholars?

The scholars use them to study the meaning of words and of grammatical forms, as well as to ascertain the precise original text. The translators of the Revised Standard Version, for example, have at many points chosen a phrase from one or more of these ancient translations—most often the Septuagint—as a correction to the Hebrew. These variations are all footnoted, and it is illuminating to study the notes and see the differences.

## 28 When was the Hebrew Bible first printed?

The first portion of the Hebrew Bible to be printed was the Psalms, published in 1477, some twenty-five years after John Gutenberg produced his Latin Bible as the first book printed from movable type. Other portions were issued in the next few years. The first complete printed edition came out in 1488 at Soncino, near Milan. After several others had appeared, a scholar named Jacob ben Chayyim prepared a four-volume edition, published at Venice in 1525-26, which has been substantially the standard Hebrew text ever since. Later scholars have had to make only minor corrections.

Previous to the above-mentioned dates, of course, every copy of the Hebrew Bible from Ezra's copy on down had to be written by hand. The copy of Isaiah on the desk of the synagogue in Nazareth from which Jesus read when he preached there was a scroll made by hand.

## 29 What version of the Old Testament did Jesus read?

Some of the synagogues in Jesus' day used an order of worship in which a lesson was read from the Law followed by one from the Prophets, just as many Protestant churches use a lesson from the Old Testament and another from the New Testament. The language of the common people in Palestine was Aramaic, a dialect sufficiently different from the Hebrew text that some interpretation was necessary if the people were to understand the reading. Just what manuscript was used in the synagogue in Nazareth is not known, of course, but it was a Hebrew text. The Septuagint had been in use for many years when Jesus was born, but there is no evidence to show that he spoke Greek; and when, in the course of his preaching, he quoted scripture he undoubtedly used a translation in which the Hebrew had been brought over into the Aramaic understood by his hearers.

## 30 Were the Writings used in the synagogue services?

It is difficult to know in just what manner the Writings were

15

used in public services in Jesus' day; for the records are just a bit hazy, and the custom seems to have varied from one synagogue to another. Some of the Psalms were used, of course, and some books like Esther were read on special days. But the Writings had not yet risen to the same dignity as the Law and the Prophets. Chronicles, Esther, Ecclesiastes, and the Song of Solomon were debated hotly for many years, even after Jesus' death. It was not until toward the close of the first century of the Christian era that the Jews reached any official agreement on the subject of the exact contents of their Bible. At the Council of Jamnia held about A.D. 90—some authorities fix the date as 91—some action was taken; but all records are lost, and the exact nature of that action cannot be determined. It is probably safer to say that no formal action was ever taken, but that the various books established themselves in popular favor and finally came to be accepted as scripture by common consent. Their final choice was the result of the impress of the Holy Spirit of God upon the minds of the people who read the books.

## 31 When were the Prophets accepted as scripture?

Again it is impossible to fix dates. We know from some non-canonical writings that it was generally agreed in 180 B.C. that the fifteen prophets we find in the Old Testament were "inspired"; for "Jesus, the Son of Sirach," writing in that year, recognized them as such and mentions the order in which they appear. The minor prophets are already grouped in the Book of the Twelve and the author of the book of Daniel refers to a collection of books which includes the words of Jeremiah (Daniel 9:2). As in the case of the Writings it must be assumed that the Prophets established themselves in popular esteem as scripture by their own power to inspire the readers.

## 32 How was the matter finally decided?

Apparently it was decided by popular opinion, followed by official action of which no record remains. Tradition says that Nehemiah brought the books of the prophets together in the first collection (II Maccabees 2:13), and it is possible that he was in some way active in the matter, but of that we have no proof. The question was settled in the case of some books when they

16

were translated in the Septuagint version, but the whole procedure is vague, and only a little is known. In the case of the Law, however, we find ourselves on solid historical ground.

## 33 When was the Law accepted as scripture?

It is strange but true that our best authenticated dates in connection with the development of the Old Testament are among the earliest. One would naturally expect that the later dates would have been more carefully preserved, but such is not the case. The record seems clearest in the case of the proclamation of the Law, about the year 400 B.C. To understand this situation we must make a brief study of Ezra. It will be necessary to make a detailed study of the book of Ezra later in this series, but our interest just now is in the part he played in introducing the Book of the Law, which became the Pentateuch in our Old Testament.

## 34 Who was Ezra?

He was a highly trained Jewish scribe who headed a mass movement of Jews returning from their exile in Babylonia to Jerusalem.

## 35 What did Ezra have to do with the Pentateuch?

He carried with him out of Babylonia a "Book of the Law of Moses" when he made his grip to Jerusalem, and as a result of his persuasion the Jews adopted it as *their first Bible*. This book was the Pentateuch substantially as we have it in our Old Testament.

## 36 When did he make his trip?

There is some confusion concerning the exact date. It is said to have been "the seventh year of Artaxerxes the king" (Ezra 7:7), but there were two kings by that name. If Ezra set out during the reign of the first, the date was 458 B.C.; but various good reasons now incline scholars to believe it must have been the later one, which fixes the date at 397 B.C. For convenience' sake the time is often referred to in round numbers as 400 B.C.

## 37 What was Ezra's authority?

He was commissioned by the Persian king then ruling in

17

Babylon to go to Jerusalem on a special errand, partly in the service of the monarch andpartly in the service of the Temple system. His credentials authorized him to (1) make an investigation of conditions in Jerusalem, (2) appoint judges over the Jews living west of the Euphrates, (3) instruct the people in the law of Yahweh and provide penalties for those who refused to obey, (4) take with him any Babylonian Jews who might wish to go to Jerusalem, (5) solicit funds for the Temple among Babylonian Jews, (6) carry the personal contributions of the king and his counselors, (7) provide for worthy services in the Temple, and (8) free the Temple clergy from taxation. This commission made him for all practical purposes the political and spiritual dictator of the Jerusalem Jews.

## 38  How much of a movement did he head?

A large company of people assembled along the banks of the river Ahava, which was one of the great canals of Babylonia (Ezra 8:1 ff.). The funds raised from all sources amounted to a tidy total, and to provide safe transit for it was a grave responsibility. The official sanction given to his enterprise and the credentials he carried endowed the expedition with great dignity.

## 39  How was the expedition received in Jerusalem?

It must have been the occasion for great rejoicing among the Jews, for the caravan brought considerable numbers of fresh colonists, considerable property, a sizable sum of ready cash, and not a few men of wealth, influence, and piety. Not the least cause for rejoicing was the evidence of imperial favor in the form of gifts for the Temple. There were those, however, to whom the enterprise seemed ominous.

## 40  What reason was there for alarm?

The Hebrews left behind in the deportation of 586 B.C. had been the poorest of the land. Jeremiah had expressed himself very frankly at the time (Jeremiah 24:2 ff.), saying that the hope of the nation lay with the Exiles. During the years that followed, life had sunk to low levels in Judea, and those who first returned found themselves slumping into the vagabond ways of the land. The immigrants who went with Ezra faced a serious situation, first in holding out against the temptations of Judea, and second in trying to lift the common levels of existence.

## 41 What happened when they arrived?

For three days the immigrants rested from their four months of hard travel. On the fourth day the vessels of gold and silver were turned over to the Temple authorities, the cash was counted and duly certified, and huge sacrifices were heaped upon the altars as sin offerings. Thereafter certain documents from the king were delivered to the proper persons. But the crowning event was the proclamation of the Book of the Law as the accepted constitution of the land (Nehemiah 8:5 ff.).

## 42 When did this happen?

It had been noised about in the Jerusalem community that Ezra had brought with him a book of the Law, but by a skillful play on mass psychology he reserved all announcements until interest had developed to a high pitch. Finally, in response to a popular demand (Nehemiah 8:1), he brought it forth some thirty days following his arrival, and read it to the people in a service which was attended by the utmost seriousness.

## 43 How was this arranged?

A vast multitude of the people was assembled in a broad open space near one of the city gates. With six Levites on each side, and with the book open before him on a wooden stand, Ezra stood ready to read. When all was in readiness, the people arose, lifted up their hands as they said Amen to Ezra's blessing, and then "bowed their heads and worshiped Yahweh with their faces to the ground" (Nehemiah 8:5 ff.). With that the reading began.

Ezra read until his voice failed, and he was succeeded by one of the assisting Levites. As each sentence was read to the people, it was explained by one of the attending Levites (Nehemiah 8:8). In the midst of the reading a terrible sense of sin and failure took possession of the people, and they broke out with loud lamentations. At this point Ezra was under the necessity of assuring them that they still enjoyed the favor of Yahweh (Nehemiah 8:9 ff.) and that they should rejoice and not weep.

The next day a group of leading citizens were brought together more or less privately to hear more from the book. To these, directions were delivered concerning the proper observance of the Feast of the Tabernacles (Leviticus 23:24, 40, 42), and steps were taken immediately to see that these instructions were carried out. The people were sent to the hills to get boughs from the trees for decorating the Temple and the city, and for seven days they feasted and rejoiced. On the eighth day a holy convocation was held.

At a stated period on each day Ezra appeared to read some section of the Law, and the Levites explained its implications. On the twenty-fourth day of the month a fast was proclaimed, and for three hours the Book of the Law was read in the presence of all the people. Then in a solemn ceremony the people were summoned to accept what they had heard as the law and constitution by which they were to be governed. One by one the elders came forward and on behalf of all the people signed the agreement publicly and thereby bound the nation to obey the law. Their signatures were confirmed by a popular oath taken by all the people, including the women and the children (Nehemiah 9-10). Perhaps the most revolutionary act of all was their unanimous agreement to tax themselves for the maintenance of the Temple services and other functions. *The first Jewish Bible was accepted by the people by their own vote.*

## 44 Had the Hebrews had no book of law theretofore?

The small Book of the Law found in the Temple in Josiah's day (621 B.C.), consisting of the major portion of Deuteronomy (chapters 5-26; 28), had been proclaimed by the good king as the law of the land, divinely given, and it had been ratified as such by the people. Copies had circulated among the Jews of Judea and Babylonia during the Exile, but it seems to have had no more than nominal authority. During some years previous to the fall of Jerusalem it seems to have been almost completely ignored by kings and governments. For practical purposes it can be said that the ceremony over which Ezra presided marked the beginning of constitutional government among the Jews and launched the Bible as scripture.

**45** **Had this new book been accepted by the Babylonian Jews?**

There is no record in existence which throws any light on that question. It is reasonable to believe that at least a considerable section of the Babylonian Jewish community looked upon it as being authoritative, but of this there is no proof beyond the fact that Ezra carried it with him to Jerusalem and proclaimed it as an instrument divinely inspired and approved by Yahweh.

**46** **How did it come into Ezra's hands?**

It was the work of Jewish scholars who lived as exiles in Babylonia and was probably more or less current among devout Jews of Ezra's day. As one of the prominent citizens of the Jewish group, and as a learned student of the nation's literature, Ezra was a man who was very apt to own a copy as a personal possession. It is quite possible that he took part in the compilation of the book, at least in its last stages. Of that, of course, we have no precise information.

**47** **Who wrote the Book of the Law?**

It is a mistake to speak of anyone as "writing" the Book of the Law, for as it came from the hands of the Jewish scholars of Babylonia it was a compilation of material taken from numerous sources, the selections having been made probably by some sort of group agreement. As it finally came into Ezra's hands, it must have been the product of the literary efforts of a large number of minds and hands. To identify any single individual as an author is impossible, for no records are in existence. Those who worked on it and put it into its final form very evidently consulted a wide variety of sources.

**48** **What were some of these sources?**

The student will remember that the Hebrews carried a large number of books with them when they were deported from Judah to Babylonia. More than twenty are mentioned in the Old Testament (I Chronicles 29:29; II Chronicles 9:29; 12:15; 20:34; 33:18; Exodus 24:7; Numbers 21:14; Joshua 8:31; 10:13; 23:6;

24:26; I Samuel 10:25; II Samuel 1:18; II Kings 8:23; 10:34; 12:19; 13:8, 12; 14:6, 15, 18, 28; 15:6, 31; 16:19; etc.). In addition to those named, scholars are convinced of the existence of others, portions of which have found their way into our Old Testament as component parts of several books. We know that the compilers of the Book of the Kings (I and II Samuel and I and II Kings) drew heavily upon historical records current in their times which have passed out of existence, for they frankly say so. Then of course there were the sermons of the great prophets available to the compilers. Thus it is comparatively easy to reconstruct the process by which the Pentateuch came into its present form when certain conditions of the time are understood.

## 49 What are those conditions?

Ten factors contributed to the formation of the Book of the Law:
1. The freedom granted to the Jews in Babylonia.
2. Their improved economic status.
3. Their responsibility for conserving the Yahwistic faith.
4. Their hope of returning to Palestine.
5. The Babylonian scholarship with which they were surrounded.
6. The shift of religious thought among them.
7. The emergence of the priests as religious leaders.
8. The rise of the profession of scribes.
9. Widespread literary activity among the Exiles.
10. Improved relations between the Jews and the government.

## 50 What about the freedom granted to Babylonian Jews?

As was explained in Study No. 4 of this series, the Jews in Babylonia were granted large liberties. The government had no desire to make life hard for them so long as they were content to be orderly citizens. Indeed, it needed them. Craftsmen, skilled workers, and even common laborers were badly needed in an empire engaged in large-scale military operations, just as in our own day Germany needed workers from occupied lands for her factories as her own manpower became absorbed in World War

22

II. Babylonia's success was promoted as the Jews were absorbed into the usual life of the land. The empire's purpose was satisfied when the Jews were rendered politically impotent. They would never have been deported in the first place if Nebuchadrezzar could have been sure they would not become a threat to his western flank. Babylonia was quite willing to grant them large liberties so long as they did not become a military menace.

**51** What about the improved economic status?

The section of Palestine from which they had been deported was a barren land, with narrow valleys between ridges of limestone hills. The deportees found it infinitely easier to grow abundant crops on the fertile acres of Babylonia alongside the great irrigation canals, and their standard of living began to rise above anything they had ever known. The freedom granted them made it possible for the more enterprising among them to engage in commercial pursuits, and shrewd traders began to amass a modest degree of wealth. With money came leisure and an opportunity to develop at least a measure of culture.

**52** Why were the Babylonian Jews the conservers of the faith?

The original deportees came from the cultured classes. Being familiar with the teachings of the great prophets and the services of the Temple, they naturally gave strong support to the national religion. Jeremiah believed they were the hope of the race (Jeremiah 24:1-10), and in Babylonia their faith became the tie that bound them together. In the meantime the Jews of Judea were without leadership, ignorant for the most part, and utterly discouraged. The future rested with the exiles.

**53** What about the hope of the restoration?

No matter how agreeable life in Babylonia might be it could never be pleasant for the Jews, and the devout among them longed for a return to their native land. This wistfulness received great encouragement from Ezekiel (593-571 B.C.), who outlined an elaborate program for the restored community (Ezekiel 40-48), including elaborate instructions concerning the religious services to be conducted after the restoration. The total result of Jeremiah's promise and Ezekiel's preaching was an intense religious passion. The Jews never forgot they were a "people of the covenant." In time the loyalty of any Jew was tested by the faithfulness with which he held to this hope.

## 54  What about the influences of Babylonian scholarship?

Upon their arrival in Babylonia the exiles found themselves in the midst of a culture richer by far than anything they had ever known. Art, literature, and science flourished to a degree the Jews had never imagined. All this was sure to have its effect upon the thinking of the more learned ones among them.

From the time the first Hebrews were carried away from Jerusalem (597 B.C.) until the day Ezra proclaimed the law (397 B.C.) exactly two hundred years elapsed. During that time some six generations had lived and died in Babylonia, and those two centuries saw the exiles pretty well acclimated to Babylonian life. To hold aloof from the surrounding culture would have been almost impossible. It was to be expected that speech forms, literary style, theological concepts, and religious thought would seep into their minds from their surroundings. The amazing thing is that their life retained any of its strictly Jewish character. Only the fact that the Spirit of the living God stood guard can explain the ultimate result.

All this had the effect of encouraging scholarship among the Jews, and the more learned among them naturally turned to their national literature in search of spiritual inspiration. But it was inevitable that Babylonian thinking should influence them and distinct traces of contemporaneous religious thought appear in the Jewish literature of the time.

## 55  How did religious thinking among the exiles shift?

The exiles had been taught by the prophets that their misfortunes were a direct result of their disobedience. They became convinced that their hope of restored fortunes rested solely with their willingness and ability to obey the laws of Yahweh. For political as well as religious reasons, therefore, they turned passionately to a study of their national history, their religious laws, and the teachings of their great prophets, in the hope of discovering the Law of Yahweh. Their religious leaders were determined that this time the nation should make no mistake. The people must *know* the law and *obey* it. The faith of the exiles became stern, exact, and meticulous in the process.

## 56  How did the priests become the nation's leaders?

The Jews lived under the watchful eye of the Persian empire. Had they made any attempt to recover politically they would have been treated as insurrectionists. The utter hopelessness of their condition drove them to find refuge in their religion, in which they enjoyed large liberty. Ezekiel's promise of the restoration and the ancient ideal of the "covenant" became conspicuous in their thinking, and as a natural result the priests benefited. The untrained mind finds it difficult to maintain a pure spiritual ideal without some scaffolding of ritual, and the humble Jew in the Exile, struggled to keep "unspotted from the world." The ancient prophets of the eighth and seventh centuries had held ritual and ceremony in contempt, but the priests of the Exile exalted it as an aid to worship.

As the spiritual life of the deportees began to develop, the synagogues and the priests began to assume even greater importance. There was a need for rites and forms which might serve as a trellis up and over which the Jewish faith might climb. Even more significant, the priests and religious leaders, in anticipation of the day when the nation would be restored, began to draft the rules and arrange the rites which should be practiced in the new life and worship. Much of their literary work is to be found in the book of Leviticus, in a section called the "Holiness Code" by the scholars (Leviticus 17-26).

## 57  What about the rise of the scribal class?

The scribes who copied the manuscripts and scattered them throughout the Jewish community became in time expert in the material with which they dealt, and eventually professional. Inasmuch as the nation's hope of restoration depended upon the fidelity with which the people kept the Law of Yahweh, the teachers of the Law very naturally became the keepers of the nation's destiny, and the scribes became those teachers. They searched the ancient books with patience and devotion to discover, if possible, what the mind and will of Yahweh might be. In the process they became historians, scholars, and theologians. They also became a new professional religious class. There had been prophets, sons of prophets, and priests in the Hebrew religious system; but during the Exile the sons of the prophets disappeared entirely, and the scribes emerged as a special group which, in time, came to have very great influence. By keeping the Law Israel was to become a holy people, a people of God—the New Testament phrase is "a peculiar people"—and in this the scribes very naturally became religious guides for the nation, a few being priests as well (Ezra 7:1-6).

## 58 What about the literary activity among the exiles?

In many respects the period of the Exile was one of the most productive of all Hebrew history, for (1) the Exiles enjoyed easier economic conditions and had more time for cultural activities; (2) Babylonian life encouraged them to develop their literary talents and interests; (3) the religious difficulties which confronted them compelled them to think along new lines, and this inevitably produced literature.

## 59 How did their relations with the government improve?

For the first half century there was no hope of a return. Then in 539 B.C. Cyrus the Persian overthrew the Babylonian dynasty and seized the throne, whereupon a new day dawned for the subjugated peoples, including the Jews. It was a settled policy of the new king to permit deportees to return to their homes if they desired so to do, and in 538 B.C. a small company of Jews did so. For the next 140 years the Persian emperors showed them almost uninterrupted courtesy and generous treatment. By the year 445 B.C. an occasional Jew was to be found in a post of political importance inside the empire (Nehemiah 1:1-2:10), an indication that the race had risen to some political dignity. This improved state of affairs made it possible for Ezra to make his historic journey to Jerusalem.

## 60 How were the returning Jews governed?

The powers granted to Ezra were very broad, and severe

penalties were provided for any who refused to obey (Ezra 7:12-26). The system which was set up in Jerusalem was not, strictly speaking, political. Rather it was a religious state which governed the people and which, in turn, owed political allegiance to the Persian emperor. The ruling authority was to be the high priest, who was responsible for the operation of the Temple's affairs, and who owed his position to the sufferance of the emperor. He was, in the final analysis, responsible for the good behavior and political loyalty of the Jews. He ruled them by a legal code which was both religious and civil in its provisions. It was accepted by the people as divinely inspired, but it had first been approved by the emperor. The income by which the government was supported was derived from a system of offerings and taxes. According to the religious beliefs of the leaders, the Jewish people were under the authority of Yahweh, and the officers of the Temple were his representatives. All this was contemplated in the letter of instructions and commission which the emperor gave to Ezra, and this gave the Book of the Law its great significance.

## 61 What did the Jews believe the Book of the Law to be?

The nation to which Ezra read the Book of the Law accepted it as containing the laws laid down by God himself for their government. The people voluntarily accepted it and imposed it upon themselves by a popular vote, but they did so believing that it had divine authority back of it. They knew, of course, people had composed the words, but they believed the Law had originated in the mind and will of God, and that it was backed by God's authority.

## 62 Why was it called "The Book of the Law of Moses"?

Although only small portions of it can have come down directly from Moses, all of it was believed to be true to the mind and spirit of the great leader of the Exodus. The constitution of the United States fills only a few pages, but whole libraries have been given over to its interpretation. It is made up of a series of statements of principle, every one of which calls for elaborate interpretation and application. The original "Ten Words" of Moses, similarly, were no more than declarations of principles of justice and morality which were later elaborated into extensive codes. Moses himself began the process (Exodus 18:13-27), and prophets, kings, and scribes continued it. Just as we say a law is "constitutional" because it is in accord with the principles set forth in the Constitution of the United States, so during the Exile a legal code or a declaration of faith was said to be "of Moses" if it conformed to what the scribes believed his mind to have been. Since this book, then, was an interpretation of history and of Israel's relation to Yahweh according to what Moses taught, it was called "The Book of the Law of Moses."

## 63 Was there only one copy of the book?

We have no knowledge concerning the number of copies of the book which may have been in existence in Babylonia, but the circumstances under which it was read to the people indicate that Ezra brought only one copy with him to Palestine. There was nothing to prevent scribes from making copies, of course; and in view of the fact that a considerable number of scholars and scribes must have been included in the company that migrated from Babylonia to Jerusalem with Ezra, it is reasonable to suppose that several copies may have come into existence within the space of a few years by the copyist's route. It is also probable that this would be a slow development and that the number would never be large; for the parchment paper used by the ancient Hebrews was produced by a laborious and expensive method, and writing by hand with a sharpened reed pen was slow and cramped even among those who were skilled in the art.

## 64 In what form was the book published?

The writing was divided into columns, separated by a blank space, according to a description in the Jewish Talmud, of "one thumb or two fingers in width," with margins at the top and bottom of "two to four fingers" whereon comments, notes, and annotations might be written by the reader. Five such rolls were required for the Book of the Law, and this eventually gave rise to the division into the "Five Books of the Law," by which name the Pentateuch was sometimes called in the years preceding Jesus' time.

## 65 When was the Book of the Law written?

It can hardly be said to have been written, for it was really assembled through various states, being composed of portions of several books, legal codes, and documents of a religious and historical nature which had long been in existence and current among the Jews. These portions, of course, had to be edited in such a way as to make them a coherent whole, and in the process of editing a considerable amount of original material was added. The finished Book of the Law was developed into a single great work toward the close of the fifth century B.C.—perhaps shortly before 400. According to the thinking of many of the best biblical scholars, the Jewish scribes and thinkers put the finishing touches on it about that time, giving it a literary, historical, and religious unity in the process.

## 66 Who were these Jewish scholars?

No one can furnish the name of any individuals, though it is possible that Ezra may have been associated with the enterprise in its final form. The most positive comment we can make is that it was done by the most devout and faithful Jews in the Babylonian community—men of ripe scholarship, deep piety, and passionate patriotism, who believed profoundly in the power and readiness of Yahweh to restore the Hebrew nation. The religious leaders of the Jewish exiles were priests and scribes, and scholars believe that these groups furnished the editors of the Book of the Law. At any rate, they compiled the book in an effort to solve the religious problem of their generation.

## 67 How did their problem differ from that of preceding generations?

In at least six respects:

1. The prophets preached reforms to Hebrew kings and governments; the Jewish thinkers of the Exile had no access to the Babylonian government and therefore could not preach any political or economic reforms.

2. The prophets undertook to save the Hebrew kingdoms of which they were a part; the exilic thinkers preached during a day when there was no kingdom to be saved, for Judah was already destroyed. The government under which they lived was an alien power which they would have been glad to have seen overthrown.

3. The prophets preached a message they believed would save the kingdoms by developing a new type of life among the people; exilic preaching was directed to expatriates whose nation was no longer in existence and whose religious problems were personal rather than national.

4. The prophets undertook to restore an ancient faith under the authority of the government; the exilic preachers were compelled to build a faith for a future which was still politically obscure.

5. The prophets believed that the practice of social justice would enable the kingdoms to survive; the exilic preachers were helpless so far as their power to influence the policy of the government was concerned. They believed their own Jewish government could be restored if they could find the correct way of obeying the laws of Yahweh.

6. The prophets decried ritual and ceremony; the exilic preachers believed it would be of the utmost importance in the restored community.

## 68 Were there no prophets among them?

We have studied two—Ezekiel and Second Isaiah. Scholars believe that fragments from other prophetic sources are to be found in Isaiah and other of the later books. But we must look in another direction for the great contribution of the prophets to the religious life of the exiles.

## 69 What was the real prophetic contribution to the exiles?

Previous to the Exile the prophets had been at all times contending with the people and the governments in behalf of Yahweh as the God of the nation and the supreme ruler of the universe. Rebels like Manasseh were frequently in revolt, and the seepage of paganism was always evident. But during the Exile the fruitage of the prophetic teaching began to appear— the people became convinced that the prophets had been right and that Yahweh alone was their God. In the second place the prophets had insisted upon obedience to the laws of Yahweh as the nation's only hope. At all times they cried out against the disobedience of the people and their governments and condemned the national indifference to Yahweh. By the end of the Exile the priests and scribes, together with any prophets that may have attempted to speak, did not have that battle to fight. It was won. Most of the people conceded that Yahweh was to be obeyed. The inquiry now was, *"What is the Law?"*

## 70 What was the meaning of all this?

It meant that the individual Jew came to have an entirely new importance in the scheme of religion. Whereas previous to the Exile the great recorded prayers were all in behalf of the nation, now the individual was encouraged to pray for himself. People began to think of Yahweh as a friend as well as the protector of the nation. It meant that the religious teachers had to put some method or way of life within the reach of the ordinary person by which that person could become personally acceptable to Yahweh and was to make a personal contribution toward the restoration of the kingdom. Piety and patriotism became very closely linked. It meant that, with the nation destroyed and all national political identity obliterated, the religious teachers had to address themselves to individuals. As these became personally acceptable to Yahweh, and as the number of such acceptable individuals increased, the hope of the restoration became brighter.

## 71 How did they propose to accomplish this?

Broadly speaking, the task resolved itself into six major objectives: (1) The religious responsibility of the individual must be made plain to all. (2) Their individual rights as Children of Israel must be made clear, and they must be exhorted so to order their lives that they might be able to realize those rights. (3) The process by which holiness might be achieved must be made so plain that any man might find it within his reach. (4) Individuals must be urged to live "holy" lives in order to hasten the coming of the day of restoration. (5) A correct ritual must be developed for use in the glad day when the restoration would be an accomplished fact. (6) *Mishpat* (social justice) must be established as a means of enlisting the favor and help of Yahweh in behalf of the restored state.

## 72 How was all this connected with the Book of the Law?

In attempting to bring the people to an understanding of

Yahweh there was ready at hand a considerable body of literature, including Ezekiel's great outline of rites and ceremonies (Ezekiel 40–48). All this had to be interpreted in the light of the religious convictions of the exilic thinkers. Scholars, devout scribes, and priests therewith began studying the history and literature of the Jews in the hope that they might find some solution of the problem, and in so doing they developed the Book of the Law.

## 73 What was their problem?

It was a very complex problem in spite of the fact that it can be stated rather simply. Why had Yahweh allowed his adopted nation to be destroyed, and his chosen people to be carried off into exile? Having discovered the answer to that question they came inevitably to the next one: What could be done to regain the favor of Yahweh, that the nation might be restored?

## 74 What was the answer?

The answer to the first question was simple. It was born of the teachings of the prophets—*the nation had sinned and was being punished for breaking Yahweh's laws.*

## 75 Where did they find the answer?

They found it on the rolls whereon were written the messages of the great eighth- and seventh-century prophets. They found it in the little Book of the Law which had been discovered in the Temple in Josiah's day. They found it in various historical documents and ancient books which recited the acts of kings of Israel and Judah. They found it in some great books of history which had been written centuries before. They found it in the traditions that were written among the people.

## 76 How did they reach their conclusion?

By tracing the history of the nation, studying its disasters, its fortunes, and its moral attitudes, they came to believe they had found the answer. It all seemed perfectly logical: when the nation obeyed Yahweh it prospered, and when it disobeyed it suffered. Upon this principle they undertook to arrange all the facts of their national and racial history. When they brought all the evidence together and combined it, they found they had an impressive argument. They called it the Book of the Law, though it contained much more than merely historical and legal material.

## 77 What else did it contain?

There were, of course, legal codes which embodied the civil usages of the people. These, it was devoutly believed, had come down to the people from Moses. By developing these laws, applying them to specific situations, and elaborating them so that they would cover all the conditions of life they expected to find in the restored community, they provided the answer to the second question—What could be done to regain the favor of Yahweh?

## 78 Was the book then only another compilation?

There is a sense in which it may be said that the Book of the Law was a compilation, though it is much more than that. It was a compilation with a purpose, the source material being blended with original material to present a ponderous argument in behalf of a single idea.

## 79 What was that idea?

It was an effort to prove that the Jews were the chosen people of Yahweh, and that their national destiny was indissolubly linked with Yahweh's purposes, which they must further by implicit obedience. Scores of illustrations out of the nation's history were adduced to prove this single point.

## 80 What was the method used?

To the scholar who is familiar with Hebrew it is very evident that material from a number of different historical documents lie embedded in the Pentateuch, though they have been so dexterously blended that the English reader gets the impression that it is one continuous recital drawn from a single source.

## 81 How can these documents be recognized?

It is not always easy for the English reader to identify them, for some of their distinguishing characteristics have been obliterated as they have been translated into the English text. But the trained student of Hebrew recognizes them very readily, for there are certain telltale characteristics.

## 82 What are those characteristics?

There are several, but we will identify but four which are most easily recognized by the English student. A little explanation and he will be able to trace them, at least in part, in his English Bible.

## 83 What is the first characteristic?

There are large sections of Genesis and some portions of the first five chapters of Exodus in which the name "Yahweh" is used systematically. Other sections within the same limits use the name "Elohim" with equal consistency. Both names are used elsewhere in the Old Testament, of course; but their appearances in this portion of the Pentateuch seems to follow a definite plan, so that scholars became convinced many years ago that they were dealing with two different documents. Suppose, for instance, one should come upon an early history of the American colonies in which, for a considerable space, the name "Nueva España" was used as the name for the New World and then, for the space of some chapters, the name should suddenly be changed to "New England." Would it not excite curiosity? We should probably undertake to make sure that both names referred to the same land, and having done so we should be apt to conclude that one author had written the "Nueva España" section and another had written the "New England" section. At least we should decide that the two sections represented two different viewpoints. This is something similar to the thing that has happened in the case of the use of the two names for God in Genesis and Exodus 1-5.

## 84 Can the English student distinguish these names?

He can do so most easily in the American Standard Version of 1901, which always uses "Jehovah" to represent "Yahweh" of the original Hebrew. But he can recognize "Yahweh" almost as easily in the Revised Standard Version, and in most editions of the King James Version, because the substitute for this personal name is always printed in small capital letters—usually as "Lᴏʀᴅ," sometimes as "Gᴏᴅ."

On the other hand the word "God" in ordinary letters represents some form of the primitive word *el* (meaning originally any supernatural being), in most cases "Elohim." The name "Lord" in ordinary letters represents a third Hebrew name for God, "Adonai," which is a form of the word translated "lord" as applied to human beings.

Thus "God" in Genesis 1:1-2:4a indicates "Elohim", "Lᴏʀᴅ" in Genesis 12 and 13 indicates "Yahweh"; "Lord" in Genesis 18:27-32 indicates "Adonai." In combination "Lᴏʀᴅ Gᴏᴅ" in Genesis 2:4b-3:24 represents "Yahweh-Elohim," and "Lord Gᴏᴅ" in Genesis 15:2 represents "Adonai-Yahweh."

Except in this last phrase, where it would make an absurd repetition, "Lᴏʀᴅ" is the regular "translation" of "Yahweh" in the King James and Revised Standard versions. In this they follow a custom that may go back even to Ezra's day. About this time the Jews—perhaps from fear of violating the third commandment (Exodus 20:7), or perhaps from realizing that God is too big for an exclusive name—stopped using "Yahweh" in speech. Though they still wrote YHWH at times, as in Chronicles, they read it aloud as "Adonai"—"Lord." By 250 B.C. this custom was so well established that the Septuagint translators did not try to represent YHWH in Greek letters, but translated the spoken substitute instead. Most translators since have followed their precedent.

The student who is interested will find it a rewarding experience to pursue the study a little further, going through the Pentateuch and making note of the different ways the various names for God are used.

## 85 What does the use of different names indicate?

It might not indicate anything more than that the author used first one name and then another for the sake of variety, until we begin to examine the text itself. Then we discover, among other things, that Genesis 1:1–2:4a uses the name "Elohim" thirty-five times in telling the story of creation and never uses "Yahweh" once. Then we find that Genesis 2:4b–3:24, which follows immediately and also deals with the story of creation, uses the compound name "Yahweh-Elohim"—believed by scholars to have been simply "Yahweh" in the original manuscript—twenty times and "Elohim" alone only four times. Again, in the five chapters of Genesis 12–16 "Yahweh" is used twenty-seven times and "Elohim" never; while in another section, 35–50, the name "Yahweh" appears but once and the name "Elohim" is used fifty-seven times. Such usage does not seem to be accidental, and certainly the names were not used interchangeably by the original authors. There must be some explanation for the fact that some sections are dominated by the one name and other sections are dominated by another.

## 86 What is the explanation?

For a good many years the matter was given no special attention. Then a French physician who made Bible study a sideline—Jean Astruc, physician to Louis XIV—called attention to this mixed use of names and suggested that Moses had consulted two different sources in writing the books. This was followed by investigations conducted by others, with the result that it is agreed today among scholars that the different names are the preferences of the different authors whose writings have gone into the compilation.

## 87 What is the second characteristic?

There are certain repetitions in the narrative which call for an explanation. There are duplicate reports of the acts of creation (Genesis 1:1–2:4a; 2:4b-25). A careful reading of chapters 6–9 of the book of Genesis reveals the fact that we have here two accounts of man's wickedness and God's displeasure. Some passages speak of *one* pair of every kind of animal being taken into the ark, while other passages speak of the "clean and unclean" and state that *seven* pairs were preserved in the case of the *"clean."* Obviously these are two different versions of the same story. Some verses say the flood lasted forty days and others that it lasted one hundred and fifty days—more evidence to the same effect. Duplicate or parallel accounts of other events are found scattered through the various chapters. There are two accounts of the promise to Abraham (Genesis 17:16-19; 18:9-15). The father-in-law of Moses is referred to under two names (Exodus 2:18; 3:1), and there are two different accounts of the sending of manna and the quails (Exodus 16; Numbers 11).

## 88 What is the explanation of all this?

The preceding paragraph does not exhaust the list of repetitions by any means, but it provides illustrations of the reason why scholars believe they are dealing with two or more different accounts of the same circumstances when they read the books of Genesis and Exodus. Similar duplications with different details carry on into the book of Judges.

## 89 What is the third characteristic?

As a careful study is made of the various legal codes it is noted that there is a certain progress being made, both in social standards and in civil provisions. A careful study of the entire Pentateuch reveals the fact that there was a growth in legal procedure, problems, and concepts running through many centuries.

## 90 What is the explanation?

As the nation developed it became necessary to enlarge the scope of the law. In the primitive life of the desert it was not necessary to have elaborate regulations concerning land and money, but once the people had passed from nomadic to agricultural life an entirely new set of conditions arose requiring new laws. Then when the exiles began planning their return to Judea, a new system of laws became necessary whereby life in the new community could be governed. This natural process and the evidence of different standards and procedures outlined in the Pentateuch compelled the scholars to conclude that they were dealing with different legal codes which originated in different periods of the nation's history. Instead of the traditional idea that all the laws of the Pentateuch were composed by Moses in the wilderness, the realization grew that many of them must have been formulated as circumstances arose requiring them.

## 91 What is the fourth characteristic?

There are different theological concepts which become apparent when we make a close study of the Pentateuch. Let us look at the primitive concept of God in the second creation story (Genesis 2:4b-25). The "Lord God" is reported to have *formed* man and other creatures, to have *breathed* into man's nostrils the breath of life, to have *closed up* the opening in man's side after taking out the rib from which he *built* the woman. All this indicates that the writer was thinking in terms of a very human God, as a primitive thinker might. In comparison with the more exalted concept of God found in the first story (Genesis 1:1–2:4a) the second is very clearly the more primitive and, it seems reasonable to assume, much older. There are other differences which will appear in later questions, but enough has been suggested to indicate the kind of evidence with which the scholars deal.

## 92 How many documents can be traced in the Pentateuch?

There is some disagreement among students in this field, of course, but there is general agreement that there are at least four, to which have been given the names "J," "E," "P," and "D."

## 93 Why such strange names?

The identity of the original authors of the documents has never been established, and these four letters are used as symbols for the more complete and less convenient names— Yahwistic (Jehovistic), Elohistic, Deuteronomic, and Priestly. Each has certain characteristics all its own, each has a purpose all its own, and each served the cause of religion in a way all its own.

## 94 What are the characteristics of the J document?

Students who are familiar with the original Hebrew will find more than the list here given, but these can be observed by the English student.

1. "Yahweh" ("LORD") or "Jehovah" is the name used for God from the very beginning.

2. As this indicates, people are assumed to have known the name "Yahweh" before Moses appeared as a leader of the Hebrews.

3. "Sinai" is the name given to the mountain whereon the Law was given to Moses (Exodus 16:1; 19:1; 11, 18, 20, 23; 24:16; 31:18; 34:2, 4, 29, 32; Leviticus 7:38; 25:1; 26:46; 27:34; Numbers 1:1, 19; 3:1, 4, 14; 9:1, 5; 10:12; 26:64; 28:6; 33:15, 16; Deuteronomy 33:2; Judges 5:5).

4. "Israel" is the name of the third patriarch following the birth of Benjamin.

5. "Canaanites" is the name used to designate the original inhabitants of Palestine at the time of the Hebrew invasion.

6. "Aram Naharaim" is the name for Mesopotamia.

7. "Egypt" is used as the equivalent of "Egyptian."

8. God appears in person to several individuals.

9. Certain characteristic phrases appear, such as: "call upon the name of," "ran to meet," "took him a wife," etc.

## 95 What are the characteristics of the E document?

1. "Elohim" ("God") is used as the name of God until the call of Moses, and frequently thereafter.

2. E assumes that the name "Yahweh" was revealed to Moses in the wilderness and was not known to people before that time.

3. "Horeb" is the name given to the mountain where Moses received the law (Exodus 3:1; 17:6; 33:6; Deuteronomy 1:2, 6, 19; 4:10, 15; 5:2; 9:8; 18:16; 29:1).

4. "Jacob" is used in preference to "Israel" (Genesis 32:32 forward).

5. "Amorites" is the name by which the original inhabitants of Palestine were known at the time of the Hebrew invasion.

6. "Jethro" is the name of Moses' father-in-law.

7. Elohim does not appear in person, but in dreams, visions, or through other means of communication.

8. Among the characteristic expressions are "the man Moses" and "bring up" (from Egypt) instead of "bring out" as in J.

## 96 What are the characteristics of D?

1. D follows E in the use of "Horeb" as the name of the mountain on which Moses received the Law.

2. Some of the characteristic phrases are: "that your days

may belong," "a mighty hand and an outstretched arm," "the sojourner, the fatherless, and the widow," "remember that you were a slave in Egypt," "do what is right [or evil] in the sight of Yahweh," "with all your heart and with all your soul," and "be careful to do."

3. Other special characteristics of the laws set forth in D will be studied later when we come to examine the Deuteronomic Code.

## 97 What are the characteristics of P?

The linguistic characteristics are very numerous. One scholar makes note of at least fifty unusual words or expressions, many of which appear nowhere else in the Old Testament.

1. "Elohim" ("God") is used as the name for God until the time of the call of Moses.

2. "Paddan Aram" is the name used for Mesopotamia.

3. P follows J in using the name "Sinai."

4. Certain forms of pronouns—understood only by students of Hebrew—are very conspicuous.

5. Certain characteristic expressions are to be observed, such as: "be fruitful and multiply," "that very day," "by their families," "soul" (meaning "person"), "throughout their generations," "congregation of the people of Israel," "breathed his last and died, and was gathered to his people."

## 98 Where did the J document come from?

For several reasons scholars believe it was written in Judah, perhaps about 850 B.C. This date is, of course, only an approximation, for there are no exact data upon which to make positive statements. The ideas expressed, the language used, the concepts with which it deals, and other reasons less obvious to the average reader, but which are significant to the scholar, lend credibility to that date. It will be remembered that it was about this time that Elijah was active in the kingdom of Israel, preaching and defending peasants against the king in their rights to remain in possession of their own lands. It was a stern, rough, and ready age, in which issues were clear and speech was frank.

## 99 Why is it believed the J document was composed in Judah?

Because the patriarch Judah appears conspicuously in the narrative, because the home of Abraham is fixed at Hebron, which is in the south (Genesis 35:27), and because the writing reflects the spirit and times in the southern kingdom as of about 850 B.C.

## 100 Did the author of J originate his material?

Ancient tales concerning the origins of the Hebrew race were current among the people from the beginning, and the author doubtless appropriated such material as was convincing to him. Some of these early stories may have been in written form, and others were doubtless told as stories. The priests recited stories connected with the various sanctuaries and taught the people the historical lore of the nation. The shepherds told stories to their children about the campfires, as did also the farmers andcity-dwellers inside their family circles. Then there were wandering bands of storytellers who carried tales from one section to another. All this material was available to the author of J, besides some written records the exact nature of which we do not know. It must be remembered that he was dealing with a body of material that was the common property of all Hebrews of that period. Roughly speaking, it fell into two general classes.

## 101 What were those two classes of material?

1. There were, first of all, the hero tales of the nation, in which the great names of the past were preserved in stories of their deeds, their conquests, their services, and the laws they had given to the nation. Much of this was very old, and the further back it went the more vague and incomplete it became.

2. In the second class of material there were stories that undertook to tell of the origins of the world and of life as it was known to the people of that day. Some questions are asked by all people: What started the universe? Where did we come from? When did we begin? Even the most primitive person has found these questions arising, and among all races there have been those who have tried to answer them. Among the Hebrews the answers took the form of stories, which some

scholars believe were gathered up in a very early book. They think that the author of J depended upon this as his written source, but the question is debatable. The earliest ground upon which we have any sense of surety is the statement that the author of J made use of material which was ready at hand and by a process of selection produced his book.

## 102 Are there no eyewitness reports in the Pentateuch?

Some events are reported in the book of Genesis which happened before man came into existence. Obviously there could be no eyewitness report in such a case. Stories like those of Adam, Noah, Abraham, Jacob, and Joseph do not profess to be reported by witnesses. When we come to Moses and the great events of the Exodus, contemporary written records would seem more likely; and in fact there are several references to Moses' writing (Exodus17:14; 24:4; 34:27; Numbers 33:2; Deuteronomy 31:9, 24). But the scholars have found good reasons for believing that few if any of the records in the Pentateuch were in written form before about 1000 B.C. During the earlier years they were passed from one generation to another in oral form. The reader must keep in mind that this was the standard method of education among all peoples of that time. True, permanent historical records were kept on clay tablets and stone monuments among the Assyrians, Babylonians, and Egyptians; but popular education in all lands was by word of mouth.

Following Moses' death events of enormous importance occurred, elaborated laws were provided for the government of the people in the midst of increasingly complicated situations, and additional legal processes were devised to deal with situations which did not exist in Moses' day. Any of this which could be made to serve his great major purpose was preserved by the author of J in his book.

## 103 Is J to be found only in the Pentateuch?

Very definite traces can be found in Joshua, and possibly in Judges, but it is in Genesis and Exodus that the evidence lies out plainly on the surface. Much J material seems to be embedded in the book of Numbers, but it is difficult to separate from material drawn from other sources.

## 104 How much does J cover?

The author seems to have begun his story with creation and continued on down to the time of the establishment of the Hebrew monarchy under King Saul. His entire work was an epic, the history of a people against a backdrop of all creation.

## 105 Where can the English student find J in the Old Testament?

It cannot be said that the following list is a complete one, for it is often difficult to separate the J material from other matter, but it will give something of an idea of the original work. It is suggested that the student obtain an inexpensive copy of the Bible and cut out the passages listed, pasting them together so as to get a view of the original composition.

J was profoundly interested in the story of beginnings, and in this interest all men share. The first great division of his book was an effort to trace those beginnings, and therein we discover the basic philosophy by which he was guided. He believed that God was the Creator of all things, and that God's guiding hand had directed in the formation of the universe, in the ordering of life, and in the fashioning of human institutions. He told it all in a story form, but deep underneath the story was his religious faith. Trace the story, then, in Genesis 2:4b–4:25; 6:1-8; 7:1-5, 7-10, 12, 16b, 17b, 22 f.; 8:2b,3a, 6-12, 13b, 20-22; 9:18-27; 10:8-19, 21, 24-30;11:1-9.

J then turned to the origins of the Hebrew nation, and gave a history of Abraham, its progenitor. God had created the universe, and now began the process of raising up a nation. His account appears in Genesis 11:28-30; 12 (except 4b, 5); 13:1-5, 6b, 7-11a, 12b, 13, 18; 15:1-11, 17, 18a; 16:1b, 2, 4-8,11-14; 18:1-16, 20-22a, 19 (except 29).

Second of the great patriarchal fathers of Israel was Isaac, whose story appears in Genesis 21:1a, 2a, 7, 33; 22:20-24; 24; 25:1-5, 11b, 18a; 26:1-33.

Between Israel and Edom, another Semitic nation, there was great rivalry in spite of their kinship. The ancestral feud between them J explains at some length, careful to show that Israel, as the descendant of Jacob, is Yahweh's favorite. The story occurs in Genesis 25:21-26a, 28; 27:1-10, 14 f., 17, 18a,

20,24-27a, 29b-32, 35-39a, 40a, 41-45; 28:10, 13-16, 19a; 29:2-14, 26, 31-35; 30:9-16, 20b, 21,24b, 25, 27, 29-40ac, 41-43; 31:1, 17, 18a, 25,27, 31, 43 f., 46, 48, 51-53; 32:3-7a, 13b-22a, 23a, 23b-29, 31 f.; 33:1-17a; 34, 35:21 f.; 36:15-19, 31-39; 38.

There are those who say that the Joseph story is the most perfect tale in all the Old Testament. J presents it in much detail, beginning in Genesis 37:3 f., 12, 13a, 14b, 18b, 21,23a, 25-27, 28b, 31a, 32 f., 35; and then continuing Genesis 39:1ac, 2-23; 42:2, 4b-7, 27,28a, 38; 43:1-13, 14b-23a, 24-34; 44; 45:1a, 2, 4b, 5a, 9-11, 13 f., 19, 28; 46:1a, 28-34; 47:1-5a, 6b, 12-27a, 29-31; 48:2b, 8a, 9b, 13 f., 17-19; 49:2-27, 33a; 50:1-11, 14, 18, 21, 24.

The history of the Hebrew people actually began with Moses, and this record constitutes the third great division of J. The story of Moses' early life appears in Exodus 1:6, 8-12, 14a; 2:11-23a; 3:2-4a, 5, 7-9a, 16-18; 4:1-16, 19, 20a, 24-26, 29-31; 5:3, 5-23; 6:1. The story of Israel's escape from Egypt begins with the account of the seven plagues: (1) the Nile is made foul (Exodus 7:14, 16, 17a, 18, 21a, 24 f.), (2) the land is overrun with frogs (8:1-4, 8-15a); (3) flies torment the people (8:20-32); (4) then murrain (9:1-7); (5) hail (9:13, 17 f., 23b, 24b, 25b-29a, 33 f.); (6) locust fill the air and destroy growing things (10:1a, 3-11, 13b, 14b, 15ac-19, 24-29); (7) death of the first-born (11:4-8).

The most impressive event in the initial history of the Hebrews, and one that colored all the thinking of the race for hundreds of years was the deliverance at the Red Sea. J reports this in Exodus 12:21a, 27b, 29-34, 37-39; 13; 3a, 4, 6, 10-13, 21 f.; 14:5 f., 10a, 11-14, 19b, 20b, 21b, 24a, 25, 27b, 28b, 30; 15:1; including the promise of the land which was to be theirs, 15:22-25a, 27; 17:3, 2b, 7ac; 18:7, 9-11.

Then came the postponement of their entrance into the Promised Land, the story of which J tells in Numbers 10:29-33; 11:4-13, 15, 18-24a, 31-35; 12:16; 13:17b, 18b, 19, 22,27a, 28, 30 f.; 14:1c, 3, 8, 9b, 31, 41-45. There follow a number of records of individual events of varied interest and theme; fragments of J appearing, some scholars believe, as far as Judges 21:15-23.

## 106    Why is it so scattered?

Because of the way it was combined with the other documents, as will be explained later. In each successive combination the compilers seem to have done their work mainly by a sort of "pastepot and shears" method, using first a portion of one and then a portion of another—sometimes in pieces of just a sentence or even a phrase in length. In a few instances along passage from one document separates what must have been originally parts of a single sentence in another.

## 107  What was J's purpose in writing?

He seems to have had a double purpose: (1) he wanted the people to understand Yahweh, the God of the Hebrews, and (2) he wanted them to understand the divine purpose that underlay their whole history.

## 108  Did J create his material?

When the Hebrews came out of Egypt they were fresh from slavery, and when they entered Canaan they were only one generation removed. In Palestine they found themselves surrounded by a culture reaching far back into the centuries, a part of which was a well-developed theology. It was perfectly natural, then, that the Hebrews, knowing practically nothing about the idea of God, should absorb much of the Canaanite thought. Their religion became mixed with pagan ideas, and pagan tales were told around their campfires. This will explain traces of Canaanite material in J. Like any other author, he drew upon all his background when he wrote, and may have found it difficult to identify original material and borrowed material.

## 109  What do we mean by traces of Canaanite material?

We know, for instance, that there were creation stories, tales of a flood, and other primitive legends current among all peoples of the East. Some Babylonia myths have been preserved for us to this day. It would have been impossible for the Hebrews to have mingled in the East without hearing these stories. If they were of a curious mind at all, they would listen with great interest, for these stories were explanations of matters about which they must have done much thinking. That they were inadequate answers must be confessed freely. But they were answers, and as such they were of absorbing interest to the Hebrews, who must have heard them for the first time. J was not satisfied with them as he found them. They did not explain the world to him satisfactorily. They did not answer the questions he was asking, but in spite of their inadequacy he could use them.

## 110 How?

Just here we discover something of the magnitude of the mind of this unknown author. He was a religious philosopher who thought ahead of his times. He believed all of life and history could be explained in terms of Yahweh, and by adapting these stories from the ancient East, giving them a deep spiritual meaning, and attributing creative action to God (Yahweh), he could make the Hebrews see that Yahweh was responsible for their world, and that as a consequence they should obey him. He therefore took the ancient stories much as a gardener takes a stick and uses it as a trellis for a vine, being interested in the stick only insofar as it will serve the vine. Thus he took the ancient stories of Canaan, rewrote them to suit his great major purpose, and then attached truths about God to them and gave them to his people. He was not interested in the stories so much as he was interested in presenting the idea of God, and the stories helped him to do that.

## 111 Where did he get his ideas?

In asking this question we are going to the very root of the whole matter of writing scripture—the work of the Holy Spirit.

## 112 What did the Holy Spirit have to do with it?

Many Christians are apt to think of the Holy Spirit as having come into existence with the advent of Jesus and the launching of the Christian Church. But Christians who understand the meaning of the doctrine know that the Holy Spirit has been active from the beginning. In some way, the precise details of which are not known, the Holy Spirit found his way into J's mind—as also into the minds of others who wrote scripture—and by some method, infinitely gracious and gentle, led them to discover divine truths. Thus, by leading, guiding, directing, and revealing, he has brought men through to an accurate and inspiring knowledge of God.

46

## 113 What happened to the revelation?

Once a mind like that of J conceived the idea of God's guidance of a race like Israel, and of the management of the historical process for a great spiritual purpose, then that mind undertook to find devices by which to communicate his "vision" to his fellows. Down through the ages great souls who have come upon great truths have used the noblest powers at their command to express those things which have become plain to them. And as the years have gone by, each has profited by the efforts of those who have gone before. Music, art, and science are all more expressive than in an earlier day when primitive men tried to express themselves. Similarly, the expression of religious truth has risen to a higher level than was common when the first religious idea broke through to the consciousness of men. This advance is evident in the Bible. Sections of the New Testament are far away ahead of anything in the Old Testament. J's great literary work remains a monumental achievement in the field of religion, in spite of the fact that it represents an early discovery of God, made by an amazing mind, under the guidance of the Holy Spirit. His literary devices may be primitive, but no one has ever conceived a greater truth than that God is the author of the universe and that man must serve him.

## 114 Was J's work the only one of its kind?

At the time J wrote there was nothing else like his book in any literature in all the world. Herodotus, the Greek who has been called the Father of History, wrote more than four centuries later. J's was the first comprehensive history of mankind, the universe, and a race that was everwritten. The Greeks have been called the great scholars of the ancient world, but they had nothing like J until hundreds of years afterward. J's work was the achievement of a master mind who thought of all history as an expression of the purposes of God.

## 115 What were his great ideas?

He grouped all his thinking around two foci: (1) he saw God at work in all of history and all of the universe; and (2) he saw man as sinful, disobedient, and a creature who was cutting himself off from Yahweh's gracious benefits by his sin.

## 116 What kind of God did he see?

Reading his lines we immediately discover that he thought of God in very human terms. He talks about God as "molding" man out of the dust, as "breathing" into his nostrils, as "walking" in the garden at the cool of the day, and otherwise behaving as a person. In the process of creating the world God seems to be experimenting—trying first one plan and then another, as a man will who is unsure of himself (Genesis 2; 3). Yet withal J's God is a noble God.

## 117 Why call J's God noble?

Because of the noble character. Having made man, Yahweh sets about to provide for his needs. He plants a garden for him and provides it with abundance; he sees that man is lonely and provides him with a companion (2:9 ff.); when man disappoints him he continues to care for him solicitously (4:15); he is infinitely patient when man is disobedient and shows a sympathetic understanding of his creature's nature (8:21). His requirements are heavy but not severe.

## 118 What does J's God require?

He presents Yahweh as being pleased with sacrifices when they are offered aright (4:5-7; 8:20-21), and he makes a distinction between the clean and the unclean, though his chief concern is not with ritual but rather with conduct. Men are to exercise self-control (3:17), restrain their pride (11:4-8), honor their parents (9:22 ff.), be faithful to their wives (2:23), commit no murder (4:9 ff.), or other wickedness (6:5). He pays man a great compliment in putting him within reach of the tree of knowledge and risking the outcome (2:17). Mankind is at liberty to do with his life what he can (6:5) even though he disappoints Yahweh. It is worthy of special note that J always emphasizes the outstanding virtues of his heroes.

## 119 What does all this mean?

It means that a man living in the midst of primitive religion, primitive thought, and primitive morals, was able to catch a glimpse of the character of God, with the help of the Holy Spirit. It was not complete, of course, for none of the Old Testament writers ever attained to that perfection. That was reserved for the New Testament, for only in Jesus Christ have we such a portrait of God. But J was many centuries ahead of his time, and in that way was God revealed to this unknown author.

## 120 What did J think about people?

He believed people were the objects of Yahweh's supreme love and care, enjoying the status of a child of Yahweh, with all the rights of a favored creature. It was for people that Yahweh created everything. Sin, to J, was a desperately serious matter which called for some divine remedy. Moreover, it is very apparent that he pondered deeply over some of the great basic questions of life.

## 121 What were those basic questions?

J sometimes gives them a quaint setting, using stories as vehicles in which to set them forth, but he faces the essential questions frankly and fearlessly.

1. He asked, "What makes people different from the rest of the creatures?"

2. "Why do people, of all creatures, wear clothing?"

3. He asked the age-old question about human suffering— "Why do weeds and thistles grow, and why do women suffer pain at childbirth?"

4. "What is the meaning of life if death awaits us all, if the body disintegrates and turns back to dust?"

5. "Why do not all people speak the same language? What makes people differ one from another? Why are nomads so much worse off than farmers are?"

6 "What makes the seasons, the processes of nature, and the stars over our heads dependable?"

7. "What gave Israel her peculiar status with Yahweh?"

## 122 Did J believe Yahweh loves all nations and races?

When we read J's words we get the impression that Yahweh is a very benign God who has been the God of all men from the beginning. He is gracious to Lot (Genesis 19), the ancestor of Ammon and Moab, thus indicating that he is interested in those nations. He loves Hagar (Genesis 16), who becomes the mother of the Ishmaelites. He is considerate of Esau (Genesis 27), the progenitor of the Edomites. He preserves the three sons of Noah (9:19) that the earth may be populated. Throughout the entire book of Genesis the treatment of non-Israelites is considerate and kind. In Exodus, however, conditions change. Here Yahweh is severe with the Egyptians (Exodus 9:15-16) and Amalek (17:16). It is evident that J is now using different material.

## 123 What do we mean by different material?

As has already been suggested, J used the oral history of the Hebrews which was current in his times, and these stories represented the opinions of the people of about 850 B.C. They were close to Egypt, Amalek, and Canaan, and had suffered at their hands. As a religious thinker J was far in advance of his countrymen and most surely took a much more godly view of the situation than they did. He filtered those stories through his exalted mind and brought them out as interpretations of the will of God. But his mind was still colored by the passions and hatreds of his generation, and his interpretations were not entirely free from those attitudes. Concerning the pre-Mosaic stories of Genesis, however, he was less biased. His mind concerning them was more open to the Holy Spirit, and when he wrote them down they fused with the concept of Yahweh which had been revealed to him. We must keep in mind, however, that even while he was writing down sacred things he was surrounded by very human situations, and was limited in his expressions to strictly human speech.

## 124 How did these human situations affect his writing?

One illustration will suffice. When the Hebrews came out of the wilderness to take the land of Palestine, they found it comparatively easy to overrun the plains and valleys, but they were altogether unprepared to take the cities, for they had none of the enginery necessary to batter down walls. They fought only with their swords and primitive desert weapons, which were helpless against city walls. For many generations the old Canaanite cities persisted in the midst of the land. Inside the cities the great landowners lived. There, too, were the moneylenders and those who foreclosed mortgages when debts could not be paid. Life in the cities was sophisticated, and whatever luxury the land may have boasted was confined to the cities. All this conspired to create suspicion and animosity in the minds of the countrymen, and the conflict between the city and the country raged through several centuries. It was perfectly natural that J should reflect this distrust of the cities in the story of the Tower of Babel (Genesis 11:4 ff.).

## 125  What did J think about sin?

In spite of the fact that he was a very early thinker and theologian, it is probably safe to say that nowhere in the Old Testament do we find more important thinking upon this subject. He believed (1) that Yahweh's supreme purposes were good and gracious, and (2) that sin cut people off from God's mercies, making it impossible for Yahweh to do for people what he desired to do. Sin was rebellion against Yahweh. This he explains in two stories.

## 126  What is J's first story of sin?

He tells the story of the woman's adventure with the serpent, in which evil comes upon her from without (Genesis 3:1). Something puts evil into the woman's mind; it is not there originally. Her reason is induced to revolt, she is made ashamed of her obedience, a new freedom is promised her, the woman is induced to look at God as being evil, and the way is paved for a great moral revolt.

## 127  What is the second story of sin?

It is the story of Cain. The young man is not "doing well." This means that he is misbehaving, is conscious of it, and is proceeding deliberately in evil-doing. It also means that he is aware of his guilt, and when Yahweh begins dealing with him he does the natural thing—he gets angry. The author here speaks of sin as a terrible thing lurking at the door of his heart

(Genesis 4:7) ready to seize him. The young man is warned that continued evil-doing is sure to produce more trouble, but he drives on stubbornly, even going on to the point of murder (4:8), thus completing his doom. He could have been saved at any time if he had been willing to turn back in repentance. Here is a towering spiritual discovery.

## 128 What is the meaning of these two stories?

J believed that humanity itself was sinful, and he tells these two stories to describe how it became so. Something precious, he believes, has been lost to man. It was a very common belief among the ancients that the golden age of humanity was in the past, and in this belief J evidently shared, believing that man had fallen from some high estate through sinning. But as he saw the race before his eyes, he was convinced that there could never be any peace between man and evil and that man must use all the powers at his command to avoid sin. The bitter hatred between man and the serpent was only a symbol. On the other hand he was convinced that it was possible for man to avoid sin. Abel did, and others could. Here is religious faith beginning its conquest of fear. And in this we meet with a sober warning on the question of reading these stories which J relates.

## 129 Against what are we warned?

J was not so much interested in describing *how* sin had entered into the world. His chief concern was with the fact that sin *had* entered into the heart of man, and that entrance represented a supreme tragedy. The serpent was only an incident in the case; the sinfulness of sin was the important factor. He used an ancient story to warm against sin; and the essential lesson in the story of Eve's temptation is not that it came in the form of a serpent, but that it came from without, it lied about God, it deceived the woman, and it failed to keep its promise. Too many students and even teachers of the Bible have given too much attention to the incidentals of the stories and too little attention to the great essential teachings. J was not primarily interested in telling a story, but in teaching a lesson. He was not, first of all, a storyteller but a theologian. If he could have been sure that his hearers could have grasped the fact of the seriousness of sin he probably would not have worried if they had doubted the detail of the serpent.

## 130 What has J's influence been?

We have no way of knowing what his influence may have been on his own generation. It is easy to believe that he was so far in advance of his contemporaries that they missed much of the significance of the things he wrote; but we do know that his work was preserved, and this is evidence that it was appreciated. But in his brilliant stories he has profoundly affected Christian thought down to this day. In the wrappings of his theology he has conveyed to us some of the most profound religious truths with which we are familiar, and much of what J did for Judah in 850 B.C., E also did for Israel about one hundred years later.

## 131 Who was E?

He was another great thinker who lived in the northern kingdom and wrote another history of Israel which, in considerable part, parallels J's account.

## 132 When did he write?

As in the case of J, it is impossible to fix an exact date, but scholars generally believe that his book was completed about 750 B.C., which would make him a contemporary of Amos.

## 133 What period of history did E's book cover?

He did not undertake the same comprehensive study as did J. He was content to begin with Abraham—whom he calls "Abram"—and carry the account down to the time of the united kingdom. (It should be noted that neither J nor E suggests a divided kingdom.) His work is an interpretation of history, rather than a philosophy of the entire universe such as J presents in his pre-Mosaic stories.

## 134 What does he have to say about Abram?

He gives us three stories about the great patriarch: (1) the story of Sarah in Abimelech's harem (Genesis 20:1-17); (2) the story of Hagar's flight (21:8-21); and (3) the story of the sacrifice of Isaac (22:1-14,19). In each of these he shows a distinct advance over J in both his ethical standard and his theological views.

## 135 In what respect is he in advance of J?

In J's story of Sarah, Abraham lies, saying his wife is his sister. E points out that this is not an actual lie, for she is in reality his half-sister.

In J's story of Hagar, Abraham acts with a heartlessness that is repulsive to us, but E undertakes to point out some extenuating circumstances in defense of the patriarch.

In E's story of the sacrifice of Isaac he points out that Yahweh demands absolute obedience, but at the same time he is opposed to human sacrifices, which were more or less common in that day.

In the story of Jacob and Esau (Genesis 25:29-34), E undertakes to clear up certain moral questions by showing that Esau has sold his birthright, thus clearing Jacob of any charge of theft. J says that Rachel becomes pregnant because she has eaten mandrakes—generally credited in the East with being a stimulant of sex passion—but E says her pregnancy is due entirely to the favor of Yahweh (30:22). Jacob's prosperity is explained as a mark of the favor of God (31:4-16) rather than as the result of any dubious practices. In making out his case he is not above the use of humor.

## 136 How did E use humor?

Rachel had stolen her father's household gods (teraphim) which he used in divining, and concealed them by sitting upon them while in her menstrual period (Genesis 31:19, 32-35). What a ridiculous situation—*a god polluted by a woman's impurity!* Surely no one could worship such a divinity!

Again, in describing Aaron's casting of the golden calf in the wilderness he makes the priest ridiculous by his account of the affair—as if the golden calf has cast itself (Exodus 32:22-24), "just like that!" Surely no one could be expected to believe it, and thus it was laughed out of court.

## 137 Did E understand God better than J?

He avoided any use of the personal name for God until the

time of Moses, in the belief that those who preceded Moses did not know the name. E had no objection to the local sanctuaries against which the prophets protested so vigorously a few generations later. He tells the story of Jacob's burial of idols and amulets (Genesis 35:1-4), of his sacrifices at Bethel (28:18), and the building of the altar (33:20). E, however, did not believe that any idol was God, but rather only a symbol. God, he believed, dwelt in heaven and communicated with men by means of angels, who used a stairway between heaven and earth (28:12). But his story of Joseph is his great masterpiece.

## 138 What about the Joseph story?

It is a well-conceived account of a spectacular life which teaches that God works silently in the affairs of men, guiding and controlling events for the accomplishment of his own righteous purposes (Genesis 41-50).

## 139 Did E use material not used by J?

He gives numerous bits of stories concerning Moses which are omitted in J's account:

1. The rescue of the infant Moses (Exodus 1:15–2:10).

2. God's revelation to Moses at Horeb (Exodus 3:1, 4b, 6,9b-15, 19-22; 4:17 f., 20b) where Moses learned the divine name. E believed that the religion of Yahweh began with Moses, whereas J traces it back to Adam.

3. The meeting with Aaron, who became Moses' first convert (Exodus 4:2f.; 5:1, 2, 4).

4. The record of Moses' miracle-working rod (Exodus 7:15,17b, 20b, 23; 9:22, 23a, 24a, 25a,31, 35; 10:12, 13a, 14a, 15b, 20-23, 27; 11:1-3; 13:17-19; 14:7, 9a, 10b, 15a, 16a, 19a, 20a, 24b; 17:1b, 2a, 4-6, 7b, 8-16).

5. The visit of Jethro, Moses' father-in-law, and the inauguration of the Hebrew judicial system (Exodus 18, except 7, 9-11).

6. The story of the golden calf (Exodus 32:1-6, 15-24).

7. The leading of the ark (Numbers 10:33-36).

8. Complaints of the people (Numbers 11:1-3).

9. The rebellion of Miriam and Aaron (Numbers 12:1, 9-15).

10. The story of the spies (Numbers 14:39-45).

11. Dathan's and Abiram's rebellion (Numbers 16).

12. Edom's refusal of safe passage (Numbers 20:14-18, 21*a*, 22*a*).

13. The serpent of brass (Numbers 21;:4*b*-9).

14. Balak's attempt to destroy Israel (Numbers 21–24 in part).

15. Punishment of the deserters (Numbers 25:3*a*, 5).

16. Appointment of Joshua as Moses' successor (Deuteronomy 31:14 f., 23).

## 140 Is E's work confined to the Pentateuch?

In addition to the extensive quotations from E which are to be found in the Pentateuch, considerable fragments are also to be found in Joshua, and possibly also in Judges and Samuel.

The story of the conquest of Canaan, beginning with the survey of Jericho by the spies and closing with Joshua's farewell address (Joshua 24) to the people, is a remarkable bit of writing (Joshua 14:6-15; 16:1-3, 9; 17:1*b*, 2, 8, 10*b*; 18:2-6, 8-10). Then follows a history of the judges, the story of the founding of the monarchy, the choice of Saul, and the unhappy ending of his dynasty (I Samuel 1; 2:11-26; 3; 7:3-17; 8; 10:17-25; 12; 15; 16:1-13; 28:3-25; 31). In all these stories E was attempting to teach the Hebrews the essentials of faith in Yahweh.

## 141 What were these essentials of the faith?

1. Israel was obligated to be loyal to Yahweh exclusively.

2. The priesthood was important.

3. Sacrifices pleased Yahweh, but obedience was more acceptable.

4. Willingness to obey to the last detail was the service which was most pleasing to Yahweh.

5. Yahweh revealed was in dreams, or by angelic communications, rather than in person.

6. The full revelation of Yahweh had come through Moses.

7. He held the monarchy under great suspicion, believing that the people should be content to live directly under the government of God, carried on by priests.

## 142 What caused the differences between J and E?

Of course there are always differences in viewpoint between any two individuals. But, aside from personalities, we must remember that E wrote probably a century later than J. During that period there were naturally developments in religious thinking—some, no doubt, as a result of the work of Elijah and Elisha. Even more important is a factor often overlooked in Bible study. Between Israel and Judah there was a sharp feud which was reflected in numerous ways throughout their history. Just as there has been a difference in some Revolutionary War stories when told in the north or the south of the United States, so also there was a difference in the coloration of Hebrew history when told in the north or in the south of Palestine. E represents the viewpoint of the north, J the viewpoint of the south. However, it is to Judah we owe the preservation of both books.

## 143   What did Judah have to do with E's book?

When the northern kingdom was destroyed with the fall of Samaria to the Assyrians in 721 B.C., all national life of the Hebrews centered in Judah. Whatever history, tradition, or literature was to survive for later generations had to be preserved by the southern kingdom. The fact that we have E's book at all is due to the care given to it in Judah. By some process not now known the book was carried down into the southern kingdom, where for some years it must have circulated alongside of J's book. Then an interesting thing happened.

## 144   What was that interesting thing?

Scholars, priests, and prophets discovered that, while the two books overlapped in many places, each had a value all its own which should not be lost. Neither was complete in itself, and neither could be dispensed with. By combining them the best of both could be preserved. Furthermore, it would be a convenience, for one roll is easier to carry than two. Just when the combination took place no one knows, but it has been estimated as about 650 B.C.

## 145   What was the result?

In the Pentateuch we have the combined work. From the creation of the world until the time of Abraham there was only one record—J's. Therefore the Judean story was used. From that point on both stories are used, with excerpts from first one and

57

then the other to make a continuous narrative. At times both accounts of the same event are presented, as in the case of Sarah's danger (Genesis 12 being J, and Genesis 20 being E). Sometimes the editor adds a sentence or two of his own to complete the connection, as in the story of Hagar's flight (Genesis 16:9). At other times the editor adds matter of his own to make some point clear (Genesis 22:15-18; 26:3b, 4 f.).

## 146  Did JE circulate as one book thereafter?

Apparently so, and it must have been carried into Babylonia as one book, though it is quite probable the manuscripts of J and E were also carried into the Exile.

## 147  Did JE include all the material of J and E?

It is impossible to make any positive statement on that point, for no one knows, today, just what the original forms of the two books may have been. We can believe, however, that the editor of JE preserved all of each that was important.

## 148  Was JE called scripture?

The idea of scripture had not yet been born in 650 B.C. Men believed that God spoke directly to prophets, and the idea that he spoke through written words had not yet dawned upon men's thinking. Literary material was accepted, read, and appreciated, but it was not credited with having been given directly by God. It was not until 621 B.C., when the Book of the Law was found in the Temple, that words written on paper were conceded to have divine authority.

## 149  What about that Book of the Law?

The story has been told at some length in Study No. 3 of this series. Suffice it to say that during a time when repairs were being made on the Temple a book was found containing a legal code. When the book was examined by the king and his counselors, it was decided that these laws were the laws of God, and the nation was ordered to obey them by royal decree (II Kings 22:3–24:4). Thereafter it was believed that the law of Yahweh might be found in a book as well as in the spoken words of a prophet.

58

## 150. What became of this Book of the Law?

It was carried, together with other religious books and historical documents, into Babylonia by the Exiles in 597 and 586 B.C. and ultimately became a part of our Pentateuch. It appears in the book of Deuteronomy (5–26; 28) and is known among scholars as the Deuteronomic Code, or D.

## 151 Is the Pentateuch composed of J, E, and D?

These three books are included, but the Pentateuch consists of additional material as well. When the final compilation of the Pentateuch was completed, it contained certain poems and at least five other codes of laws.

## 152 What about the poems?

The Hebrews were a singing people. It is probably true that they composed more songs than any other race of antiquity. Some of these were marching songs which developed as commemorative of great events associated with their national history. No one wrote them. Like the Negro spirituals, they were the product of the experience of the race. It is possible that some of the great stories of J and E were originally sung by the people, for their present form is often somewhat poetical. But there are some excellent poems in the Pentateuch which were inserted for their own sake when the Book of the Law was finally compiled in Babylonia.

## 153 What are some of those poems?

The names of two ancient collections are preserved for us—"The Book of the Wars of Jehovah" (Numbers 21:14) and "The Book of the Upright" (Joshua 10:13; II Samuel 1:18). We have no way of knowing what they were, but some poetry in the Pentateuch may have been copied out of them.

There are, however, certain blessings in poetical form, such as Rebekah's blessing (Genesis 24:60), Isaac's blessing of Jacob (Genesis 27:27-29), Jacob's blessing of Ephraim and Manasseh (Genesis 48:15 f., 20). Then there are the Song of Lamech (Genesis 4:23 f.) and the Song of the Well (Numbers 21:17), both of which seem to be desert songs. There is the triumphal hymn of Miriam, composed immediately after crossing the Red Sea (Exodus 15:21), and the blessings of Noah (Genesis 9:25-27), the blessing of Jacob (Genesis 49:2-27), the blessing of Moses (Deuteronomy 33:6-25), all of which are early poems illustrating the type found in the Pentateuch. Perhaps the greatest of all is the familiar song of Deborah, found in Judges 5.

## 154 What legal codes were there?

There were in all six legal codes awaiting the hands of the compilers of the Pentateuch:

1. The Covenant Code (Exodus 20:22–23:33) and the Ritual Decalogue (34:10-26 and 22:29b-30; 23:12, 15-19).
2. The Twelve Curses (Deuteronomy 27:14-27).
3. The Ten Commandments (Deuteronomy 5:6-21; Exodus 20:1-17).
4. The Deuteronomic Code (Deuteronomy 12–26).
5. The Holiness Code (Leviticus 17–26).
6. Legislation of the Priestly Code.

## 155 Where did these codes come from?

They were all the product of definite historical situations, but because of an interesting Hebrew way of thinking they were all called the "Laws of Moses."

## 156 What was this Hebrew way of thinking?

It was known that there were laws which antedated Moses, such as the law of the Sabbath (Genesis 2:3), the rite of circumcision (Genesis 17:10-14), and certain rules given to Noah (Genesis 9:3-6). Then there were royal edicts put forth purely as human decrees (I Samuel 30:23-25). But in the main it was commonly believed by the Jews at the time of the Exile that no Hebrew law, whether oral or written, was binding unless it was of Mosaic origin. This belief in the Mosaic origin of all law was one of the cornerstones of Jewish faith, but our modern study of these various codes reveals a Palestinian background for much legislation which could not have been known to Moses. By the time of Ezra, however, any law to be respected by the people had to have back of it in some form the authority of Moses.

## 157 Which was the earliest of these codes?

As we have already seen in Study No. 3, the Book of the Law

found in the Temple was the first writing ever to be accepted by the Hebrews as authoritative. Though they did not call it scripture, the word not being known to them, at least in its modern sense, they did accept its commands as being from God and binding upon them. The entire book as it appears in Deuteronomy 5–26 and 28 is called the D document by the scholars; and the code of laws which it contains, the Deuteronomic Code, is the earliest written code of which we have any record.

**158** Why separate the code from the rest of the book?

A part of Deuteronomy (chapters 5–11 and 28) is a historical narrative or, perhaps more accurately, a bit of prophetic preaching in behalf of the code itself, which is to be found in Deuteronomy 12–26. A careful study of the book will reveal the difference between the two styles and types of material.

**159** Why is Deuteronomy believed to be the Book of the Law?

If the Book of the Law has been preserved for us at all, it surely appears in the Pentateuch; and no other part fits so well into the situation out of which the Book of the Law is known to have come.

**160** What was that historical situation?

The prophets were trying to lead the people back from the idolatry which had inundated the nation during the Assyrian period. They were intent on purging it of all pagan influences; and in so doing they had to get rid of Assyrian practices carried on in the Temple, the Assyrian gods which had been installed therein, and the pagan practices at the unsupervised rural altars. A major objective was the centralization of all worship at the Temple.

**161** Was this an innovation?

From the time of the Assyrian conquest, particularly, there was a considerable danger that Yahweh worship would be corrupted by the paganism with which it was surrounded. Hebrew officials, anxious to curry favor with the Assyrians, found it easy to surrender to pagan pressure. The Assyrians, on the other hand, insisted upon their own religious rites as a symbol of subjugation. The prophets sensed the danger in this tendency and undertook to counteract it. This situation is clearly reflected in the chapters of Deuteronomy. In addition, there was a social and economic situation that called for stern action.

## 162 What was that social and economic situation?

As has been explained more fully in previous studies, a sharp cleavage had appeared in the life of the kingdom of Judah with the rural landlords arrayed against the city capitalists and moneylenders. The prophets, determined to restore *mishpat* (the ancient social justice), incorporated various economic provisions into their system as a protection of the poor against the exploiters. The fact that this struggle is reflected in the legal code of Deuteronomy has persuaded the scholars that we have in D the essentials of the Book of the Law found in 621 B.C.

## 163 Why were they called the laws of Moses?

Following the ill-fated reign of Hezekiah, during which the Assyrians pillaged the kingdom of Judah, Jerusalem escaped destruction only by a miracle and by the payment of an enormous indemnity. Judah became an Assyrian vassal, and Manasseh, the king, went completely collaborationist, doing all in his power to Assyrianize Judah. Patriotic prophets, faithful to Yahweh, were hounded to earth and slaughtered in cold blood. The life of the people was debauched, and for a time it appeared that Yahwism would be stamped out.

Through the half century of Manasseh's reign, however, the faithful prophets met in secret, sustained one another's faith, and planned for the day when their land would be liberated and they would be free again to preach their Yahwistic conviction, reform the life of the land, and restore the ancient ideals of Moses. In the confidence that they were committing the ideals of Moses to writing and that they were applying his principles to the new conditions of life in the midst of which they were compelled to live, they fashioned a code of laws which were to operate the day that liberty and freedom would permit. These they called the laws of Moses. Because Huldah, the prophetess, and Joshiah, the king, recognized their code as expressing the Mosaic ideals, they were proclaimed to be the constitution and were called the laws of Moses.

## 164 Was Deuteronomy written as a lawbook?

It is perhaps better to describe the book as a sermon which included a body of laws, for its style is that of a preacher who pleads, warns, exhorts, and encourages. Let the student note the simple law of Exodus 21:2, for instance, and see how Deuteronomy explands it in true sermon form (Deuteronomy 15:12-15). Moses is represented as a prophet (Deuteronomy 18:18 compared with Hosea 12:13, also Numbers 11:4-30) and not primarily as a lawgiver (Exodus 15:25) or a priest. Jeremiah spoke rather sharply on this subject on one occasion, saying that Moses gave the people no laws or ceremonies to be observed in the desert (Jeremiah 7:21-26).

## 165 Why call Deuteronomy a sermon?

The book is a sermon in its general form, with an introduction (chapters 5–11), an exposition (12–26) listing the divine commandments, and a conclusion listing the benefits (28:1-14) and the curses (28:15-68) which will follow disobedience.

## 166 What is the main theme of the sermon?

The authors of the book believed with all their hearts that obedience to Yahweh was the only course open to the Hebrews which promised any good fortune. Both from the standpoint of personal interest and from the sense of gratitude the people must be persuaded to "keep the law." And although there is no semblance of order in the laws as they are listed in Deuteronomy, they do fall into four general groups.

## 167 What is the first group?

The religious laws comprise 150 out of the 340 verses of the entire code. First of all, worship is to be centralized at Jerusalem (12:2-28) and the high places are to be destroyed. Burnt offerings and other sacrifices anywhere else are forbidden (12:13, 17-19; 15:19-23), and the three annual feasts are to be observed only at Jerusalem in the Temple (16:1-17). One of the most interesting provisions is the one related to the privilege of slaughtering animals for food "without benefit of clergy." It was the belief of the ancients that the life principle was in the blood, and that if an animal was slain for food the blood must be given back to the god who gave the life. This meant that the local priest also became the local butcher. If all worship were to be centered in Jerusalem without some change in the custom, the rural folk would be deprived of all opportunity to eat meat, for there would be no priest to kill the animals. To meet this situation permission is given to slay animals for food without going through the sacrificial forms (12:20-24). This is in direct contradiction of the ancient custom in which butchery involved sacrifice (Leviticus 17:3 f.; I Samuel 14:32-35). As a further conciliation of the rural priests, permission is given to them to come up to Jerusalem and officiate in the Temple (Deuteronomy 18:6-8), but the record shows that Josiah was not able to put this provision into force (II Kings 23:8-9).

Civil trials were held a the rural shrines (Exodus 22:8), but the D code reorganizes the judicial system so that cases are to be heard at Jerusalem (Deuteronomy 16:18; 17:8-13). Cities of refuge are appointed whereat unintentional killers are safe as they were formerly at the local shrines (Deuteronomy 19:1-13). Provisions are made for converting tithes into money so that the people will not be burdened with the necessity of bringing their produce to the Temple (14:22-29), and a ritual is provided for the presentation of both money and fruits (26:1-11, 12-15).

To "purify" the worship further, certain defilements are put under the ban (12:16, 23-25; 14:3, 21; 15:23; 21:1-9, 22 f.; 23:9-14, 17 f.; 24:8), and such matters as mourning customs are regulated (14:1). Various "abominations" are listed (16:21–17:1; 18:9-12; 22:5; 23:18) some of which are monstrous, such as child sacrifice (18:10), and some of which are trivial, such as wearing the clothes of the opposite sex (22:5).

To keep the racial stock clean (14:1 f., 21; compare with 7:6; 26:19) there is to be no mixing with the Canaanites (12:29 f.) or the Amalekites (25:17-19). But, strange to say, the Edomites and Egyptians are acceptable (23:3-8).

Judeans who forsake the worship of Yahweh are dealt with sternly (12:29–13:18; 17:2-7; 18:20). Then there are some miscellaneous laws relative to the revenues of the priests

(18:1-8), the identification of the prophets (18:15-22), and concerning vows (23:21-23).

## 168 What is the second group?

Included in the code are a considerable number of humane laws, which fall into three classifications: (1) laws concerning the waging of war (20:5-8), (2) laws concerning treatment of the needy, and (3) laws concerning kind treatment of animals.

It is doubtful if a more humane code could have been found anywhere in the world than this one, the product of prophetic sensitiveness during the period of oppression. The alien is to be treated well (24:17 f.; 27:19), and debtors are to be shown consideration (23:19 f.; 24:6, 10-13). Justice is to be impartial (16:19), and even applies to animals (22:6 f.; 25:4).

The landless Levite (12:12, 19; 14:27, 29; 16:11, 14; 26:11-13) is provided for, the rights of hired servants are described (24:14 f.), the poor are to be fed (15:7-11; 24:19-22), runaway slaves are to be assisted (23:15), and even criminals are to be shown some consideration (25:1-3, 24:16). As a sample of prophetic concern, and as a forerunner of modern safety legislation, parapets are ordered at the edges of the roofs to prevent accidents (22:8).

## 169 What is the third group?

This is a group of civil regulations, dealing with such questions as land titles (19:14), honest weights and measures (25:13-16), contracts (15:1-11), liberating of slaves (15:12-18), punishment of immodest women (25:11 f.), certain family regulations (21:10-14, 15-17, 18-21), marriage laws (22:13-21) and definitions of sex crimes (22:22-30), divorces (24:1-5), kidnaping (24:7), local judges (16:18-20), witnesses in courts (19:15-21), and judicial procedure (21:1-9, 22; 25:1-3).

## 170 What is the fourth group?

These laws have to do with the organization of the the state, the highest court (17:8-13), the king (17:14-20), government officials (20:9), hostile cities (20:10-20), citizenship rights of eunuchs (23:1), of bastards (23:2), of Ammonites and Moabites (23:3-6), and of Edomites and Egyptians (23:7).

## 171 When did the Deuteronomic Code get into the Pentateuch?

When the exiles were carried off into Babylonia in 586 B.C., they carried the Book of the Law with them, but they also carried with them the combined book of JE, which was in many ways a sacred book among them by this time, though it had been proclaimed "scripture." Its authority among the people was due solely to its importance as a piece of written literature. Scholars believe that sometime, perhaps about 550 B.C., the two books JE and D began to be associated together in some such fashion as the Bible and the hymnbook are associated in many modern Christian homes. Then in time they came to be regarded as one.

## 172 What was the next code to develop?

The Holiness Code (abbreviated H) came into existence about the time of, or shortly after, Ezekiel's ministry.

## 173 Where is it to be found in the Old Testament?

It consists of ten chapters of the book of Leviticus (17–26).

## 174 Where did it originate?

It was probably composed by some priest, or priests, in exile in Babylonia shortly after 570 B.C..

## 175 Who were the composers?

No one knows, though there are those who believe Ezekiel was associated with it in some way. If he was not, at least he had much in common with the composers of the code.

## 176 What caused the Holiness Code to be written?

According to the common belief of the exiles, their misfortunes were a result of disobedience, as they had been taught by the prophets. Inside the Jewish community in Babylonia there were those who were determined, if possible, to discover a way to please Yahweh and regain his favor. The author of H was such a man, and the code was designed to accomplish that end. In writing he had one very definite idea.

## 177 What was the author's great idea?

He believed that Yahweh was holy and could be pleased only by a people who were holy, and Yahweh's laws were designed to promote holiness.

## 178 What did he believe holiness to be?

This is a very important question and deserves very careful attention. Among modern Christians holiness is thought of as something moral, but among the exiles—and to the author of the Holiness Code—the idea of morality was relatively unimportant. The holiness he had in mind was largely physical. It consisted of a complete separation from everything tabooed by the religion of Yahweh. It was a matter of complete dedication to Yahweh and an absolute separation from everything connected with any other god or religion (20:26). His slogan was, "You shall be holy; for I Yahweh your God am holy" (19:2; 20:7, 26; 21:8).

## 179 Was this a new idea?

Not exactly. It was an old idea among the ancients that one could win the favor of his god by observing the proper ceremonies with strict care. But "holiness," as the author of H believed in it, was something of a novelty in the religious development of the Jews. The eighth- and seventh-century prophets had insisted upon social justice as the mark of the man and nation acceptable to Yahweh. Amos and Isaiah had been particularly condemnatory of ritual and ceremony when they were offered as a substitute for just dealings. Under the influence of the Deuteronomic Code righteousness and love were identified as the characteristics which ensured the favor of Yahweh. Ritual holiness, as H described it, represented a new turn in the course of Jewish religious development, and appears definitely in the writings of Ezekiel.

## 180 How did H define holiness?

This can best be understood by studying the types of law included in H, and these can be grouped in ten classifications.

## 181 What is the first group?

Laws relative to the eating of meat (17:1-9). Here we find a sharp contrast with D, which permitted slaughtering without sacrifices (Deuteronomy 12:15, 20-22).

## 182 What is the second group?

Various laws concerning marriage and sex chastity. Egyptian and Canaanite customs are condemned (18:1-5), and various marital relations are branded as dishonorable (18:6-30). It is interesting to note that some of these are a contradiction of usages permitted in the nation's past (18:18). The basic idea, of course, is that of separateness.

## 183 What is the third group?

A description of religious and ethical duties (chapter 19). Here are parallels to the Ten Commandments (19:2-4, 11, 30), ritual suggestions (19:5-8), prohibition of pagan practices (19:19, 26-29, 31), and some moral instructions (19:13-18, 20-22, 32-37).

## 184 What is the fourth group?

Penalties for violations of the laws in chapters 18 and 19, for the practice of Molech worship (20:1-5), necromancy (20:6-8, 27), dishonoring parents (20:9), unchastity (20:10-21).

## 185 What is the fifth group?

Here are laws relative to the priesthood (chapters 21, 22).

## 186 What is the sixth group?

A definition of the sacred festivals, including the Sabbath (23:1-3), Passover (23:4-8), Pentecost (23:15-21), New Year (23:23-25), Day of Atonement (23:26-32), and Tabernacles, or Booths (23:33-43).

## 187 What is the seventh group?

A brief section telling about the laws of the sacred lamp (see Exodus 27:20) and the twelve loaves of showbread (Leviticus 24:1-9).

## 188 What is the eight group?

Another brief section dealing with punishments (24:10-23).

## 189    What is the ninth group?

An extended section dealing with the matter of the sabbatical year (25:1-7), and the year of jubilee (25:8-55). This year of jubilee was counted but, according to the rabbis' reports, never really observed.

## 190    What is the tenth group?

This is a concluding section dealing with idolatry, Sabbath observance, and curses upon those who do not observe the preceding laws (26:1-45).

## 191    Is H only ritualistic?

Not entirely. There is a nice regard for the social and moral interests of the people which is not wholly ritualistic or ceremonial. Chapter 25 is strongly social in its implications, and savors of the spirit of the eight-century prophets, and chapter 19 (verses 17 ff.) is one of the mountain peaks of Old Testament ethics. Here is an insistence that the heart, and not the deed alone, counts in the estimation of God. Jesus called a sentence from it one of the greatest of all commandments.

## 192    When did H get into the Pentateuch?

The Holiness Code seems to have been preserved as a program to be put into effect whenever the exiles were permitted to return to the Promised Land. It lay ready at hand waiting the judgment of the compilers who finally put the Pentateuch into its present shape about 450 B.C.

## 193    What is the next code to be considered?

It is known as the Covenant Code and has a complicated history.

## 194    Where is it to be found in the Pentateuch?

Exodus 20:22–23:33; 34.

## 195    Who wrote it?

The original core of the Covenant Code is the decalogue

contained in Exodus 34, but this has been edited and revised several times. It is a medley of laws governing civil, criminal, ritualistic, and moral action which seems to have been commonly accepted throughout the East about 1200 B.C., and was adopted by the Hebrews after they invaded the Land of Promise. In the process of editing it was given a Hebrew complexion, but scholars believe it goes back to the time of the Hebrew invasion of Canaan. It cannot be said to have been written by any one man, but rather it represents an ancient code current among many peoples of the East.

## 196 What was this process of editing?

Originally these laws probably did not refer to any one divinity, but were simply rules by which men lived. The incoming Hebrews took them over and ascribed them to Yahweh, and when they were written down they were adapted to the needs of the Hebrews in their new land and home.

## 197 Why was this necessary?

Because new situations developed in Canaan which were entirely outside the range of their desert experience. Questions concerning the management of unruly stock would not come up in the desert, but they did arise in a settled community. Problems of money would not arise among desert nomads who never handled money, but they would show up among a people who mixed with commerce in a crowded land. Damage to fields and other matters mentioned in the code were problems with which nomads did not have to deal.

## 198 What laws does the code include?

Laws concerning (1) persons, (2) property, (3) social customs, (4) religion.

## 199 Why is it said that its history is complicated?

Because it is impossible to say just when it first came into written form. The regulations reflect conditions prevailing previous to the establishment of the monarchy, for no king is mentioned. Because of a close correspondence between the Covenant Code and the Deuteronomic Code in many matters, it is believed the authors of D copied, or quoted from, the Covenant Code. It is sufficient for the purposes of this study, however, to say that it was preserved in written form and available to the compilers of the Pentateuch in Babylonia, and has been incorporated into the great Book of the Law.

## 200 What about the Twelve Curses?

This strange bit of scripture (Deuteronomy 27:14-26) consists of twelve solemn curses which Moses is said to have commanded should be uttered before the Hebrews at the time of their crossing of the Jordan. Strictly speaking, they are not a legal code, but a liturgy in which the people participated, the congregation repeating a response after each curse. The curses take the form of legislation because they deal with offenses which are known to God alone, and which are beyond the power of the community to punish.

## 201 Why do they appear in Deuteronomy?

They do not seem to have been a part of the Deuteronomic Code originally, but to have become attached to it during the passing of the years. Moses' order that the six tribes are to stand on Mount Gerizim (27:11-14) for the blessing and Mount Ebal for the curse became the basis of the Samaritan claim that Gerizim was the holy mountain of Yahweh (John 4:20), a claim of which much was made in Ezra's day and later. The chief interest in the twelve curses lies in the hint they furnish concerning the morals of the times.

## 202 What is indicated concerning the morals of the times?

By reading them we discover what was esteemed crime— contempt for parents (27:16), incest with father's wife (27:20), bestiality (27:21), incest with sister (27:22) and mother-in-law (27:23), moving landmarks (27:17), perversion of justice (27:19), accepting bribes (27:25), misleading the blind (27:18).

## 203 What about the Ten Commandments?

This famous bit of legislation appears in the Old Testament in two forms. D presents one (Deuteronomy 5:6-21), and a second version appears in Exodus 20:2-17, the latter being the one better known. The story of the origins of "the law of the Ten Words," and the great care taken to preserve it in its purity (Exodus 19:16 ff.; Deuteronomy 4:12 ff.) forms one of the most dramatic recitals in the Old Testament. It is a considerable problem, then, to explain the fact that two versions have been preserved, between which there are several differences. It is the opinion of many scholars that the Exodus version is the older of the two, the Deuteronomic version having been a revision made to conform to a more complicated civilization. The Deuteronomic version, for instance, inserts the word "field" into the commandment concerning coveting, indicating that the land problem has become acute. A comparison of the laws relating to the Sabbath reveals other differences.

## 204  How is this to be explained?

Hebrew history attributes the "Ten Words" (a better translation than Ten Commandments) to Moses, but we know that in at least one case David established a rule and after it had become a custom it was attributed to Moses (see I Samuel 30:21-25 and Numbers 31:25-31). This suggests that Moses must have given the basic principles of Hebrew law and as those principles were applied to specific cases they developed into a system of regulations, each individual rule being endowed with the authority of Moses. In time all traditional Hebrew law came to be called the law of Moses. When the compilers of the Book of the Law set about their work the two versions were available, and both were inserted in the book, the compilers making no effort to decide between the two.

## 205  What is the Priestly Code in the Pentateuch?

The latest system of legislation among the Jews. It consists, strictly speaking, of two types of material. A part of it is narrative and a part is legislative. But even the narratives have a legislative purpose. It is very evident that the compilers were attempting to make it serve the purpose of regulating the lives of the restored community.

## 206  How can narratives have a legislative purpose?

They are stories told for the purpose of describing the origins of religious laws, institutions, and practices, with the thought that once the worshiper recognizes the great significance and the holy beginnings of the law or institution he will be loyal to it.

## 207 Where are the Priestly narratives to be found?

There are at least thirty of them scattered through the books of Genesis, Exodus, Leviticus, and Numbers.

## 208 Which are the thirty?

1. The story of Creation (Genesis 1:1–2:4a), showing the origin of the Sabbath (2:2).
2. The story of the Deluge (6:9-22; 7:6, 11, 13-16a, 17a, 18-21, 24; 8:1-2a, 3b-5, 13a, 14-19; 9:1-17, 28 f.), and the laws which prohibit the eating of meat with the blood (the soul), also murder (9:4-6).
3. The covenant with Abraham involving circumcision (17; 21:4).
4. Abraham's purchase of the cave which gave him legal title to the land (23; also 25:7-10; 49:29-33).
5. Stories of Esau and Jacob (26:34 f.; 27:46; 28:1-9), which furnish a basis for prohibiting mixed marriages.
6. Israel's deliverance from Egypt (Exodus 11:9–12:20, 28, 40-51; 13:1 f.), with the laws relative to the celebration of the Passover and the Feast of Unleavened Bread (12:1-20), the night of watching (12:42), and the divine ownership of the first-born (13:1 f.).
7. The story of the manna and the quails (Exodus 16) in support of the Sabbath (16:23-30).
8. The ordination of Aaron and his sons (Leviticus 8).
9. Aaron's assumption of his priestly duties (Leviticus 9).
10. Punishment of Aaron's sons for sacrilege (10:1-6).
11. The blunder of Aaron's other two sons (10:16-20).
12. The stoning of the blasphemer (24:10-14).
13. The census of the tribes (Numbers 1:1-47), of the Levites (3:1-39), and the first-born males (3:40-51).
14. An example of generosity (7:1-89).
15. Installing of the Levites (8:5-26).
16. The second celebration of the Passover (9:1-13).
17. The gloomy report of the ten spies (13:1-17a, 21,25-26a, 32a; 14:1a, 2, 5-7, 10, 26-29, 34, 38), a warning against

doubting God's goodness and power.

18. Stoning of a Sabbath breaker (15:32-36).
19. Death of Korah and his followers, who opposed the exclusive Aaronic priesthood (16:1–18:32).
20. Moses and Aaron forbidden to enter the Promised Land on account of their doubts (20:1a, 2, 3b, 4, 6-8, 12).
21. Death of Aaron and choice of his successor (20:22-29).
22. Punishment of Zimri (25:6-18) for a mixed marriage.
23. The second census (26:1-65).
24. A daughter's inheritance (27:1-11).
25. Moses sees the Promised Land, and Joshua is chosen as his successor (27:12-23).
26. The Midianites are punished (25:16-18), and a new law of spoils instituted (31).
27. Allotment of territory to Reuben and Gad (32:1a,2b, 4a, 6-15, 18 f., 28-33).
28. Moses' last instructions (33:50-56; 34).
29. Allotment of forty-eight cities to the Levites, with laws concerning killings (35:1-34).
30. Some supplemental legislation relative to inheritances of daughters (36).

**209** **What is the legislative material of the Priestly Code?**

The legislation includes the revelation to Moses at Sinai (Exodus 25:1–31:18 and the laws in Leviticus 1–16; Numbers 1–10), on the journey from Sinai to Kadesh and also at Kadesh (Numbers 15:1-13, 37-41;19), and more revelations on the plains of Moab (Numbers 28–30).

**210** **When did the Priestly Code come into existence?**

It is believed to have originated between the time of Haggai and Nehemiah, or sometime between 500 and 400 B.C.

**211** **What was its original purpose?**

It was, in effect, the charter of the new Jewish church. It proposed to furnish a convincing background of narrative and legislation for the great Jewish religious beliefs and practices, upon the basis of which the rehabilitated Jewish faith could be raised.

**212** What is meant by the rehabilitated Jewish faith?

The political state was destroyed. Ezekiel had taught the people that the nation would be restored, but that its life would be organized around the Temple, rather than around the throne. This gave the Temple an entirely new standing in the life and estimation of the people.

Inasmuch as the best Judah could hope for was some status as a Persian province, without political independence, the Jewish leaders began to think in terms of a national life centered about the great tenets of their faith. God was to be their Supreme Being with priests as God's representatives, and the Torah, (the Law) God's revealed will. Very naturally this set off the Temple—its services, its management, and its ceremonies—as something unique. If it could be made acceptable to Yahweh, the nation would prosper. If not, they would come again under this wrath. In view of all they had suffered, no price was too great to pay this time, that they might be sure of Yahweh's approval.

**213** How did they set about to accomplish their purpose?

The author of the Holiness Code had laid out a program of feasts, ceremonies, and ritual which was to be established as the procedure in the restored Temple. Ezekiel's preaching had fixed the pattern. Then came the author or authors of the Priestly Code with their elaborate scheme which should, so they proposed, encompass all of life. Because of the great moral, spiritual, and social weight it was destined to carry, it was necessary that it should be, in all respects, exact and scrupulously precise. This condition gave it its peculiar form.

**214** What is that peculiar form?

Its style is formal, precise, stilted, and full of unique and characteristic phrases, which distinguish it from all other Pentateuchal literature. Genealogies, lists, statistics, exact dates, and precise measures are to be found in abundance. It is definitely and conspicuously priestly and legal in form.

**215** Why is it called the "Priestly Code"?

Because of the character or style of its presentation—being

chiefly concerned with ritual, ceremony, legalism, and cultic correctness. But it is perhaps in its historical narrative that it has exercised its deepest and most lasting influence upon modern religious thought. The author, in telling the story of Israel's spiritual heritage, attempts to teach the people the deep and lasting lessons of their faith.

## 216 How does the author proceed?

Beginning with a story of the creation of the world which is both majestic and moving, the writer undertakes to show how all the great Jewish concepts are embedded in the moral foundations of the universe. The story of creation leads up to the climax of the Sabbath, which is central in the new Jewish life. Although the Sabbath had been grossly neglected previous to the Exile, it is now to occupy the center of the stage in Jewish thought. Then comes the story of Noah, with the second great Jewish teaching.

## 217 What Jewish teaching is associated with Noah?

The whole story of the flood, with Noah's connection therewith, heads up in the laws which prohibited the eating of blood. About this principle a large body of Jewish practice and belief revolved.

## 218 What is the next great lesson?

The rite of circumcision had become a distinguishing mark of the Jews, and the author of the Priestly Code tells the story of its origin (Genesis 17), linking it up with the divine program of Yahweh. Similarly, the story is told of Israel's identification with the land of Canaan.

## 219 How is Israel identified with the land?

When Abraham purchased the cave of Machpelah at Hebron (Genesis 23), he came into possession of it by a perfectly valid and legal process. Accordingly, therefore, Israel became the rightful heir to the land. Canaan was to be the homeland of the nation, and there their ancestors were buried. They were destined to be a people apart, who were not to marry or mingle with the aliens who surrounded them. This is the teaching of

Jacob (Genesis 26:34 f.; 28:1-9) and Esau stories (36:6-8, 40-43), as well as the Joseph story (Genesis 29:24, 28-29; 30:22; 31:18; 33:18b; 35:6a, 9-13, 15; 37:1-2; 41:46a; 46:6 f.; 47:7-11, 27-28; 48:3-6; 49:1, 28-33; 50:12 f.). Thereafter the story goes on to tell how the Hebrews came into possession of the land, and Moses is introduced.

## 220 What does the Priestly documents have to say about Moses?

There is a brief account of Egypt's oppression of the Hebrews and Moses' call when the name of Yahweh is revealed for the first time—in contrast with J, which says that Yahweh was known and worshiped almost from the beginning. The great event of the Exodus is the occasion for establishing the Feast of the Passover (Exodus 12:1-14, 28), which is to be a memorial to the Jews of a significance equal to that of the Holy Communion among modern Christians. At Sinai, Moses ascends into the mountain and receives the law directly from Yahweh (24:15-18a). Again a Jewish doctrine comes to the fore.

## 221 What is this new Jewish doctrine?

The law of the sanctuary is given and the priesthood established (Exodus 25-29), and a calendar of feast days is determined (Leviticus 23:4-8, 13 f., 21, 23-28, 39). All this is for the purpose of strengthening the claims of the Temple.

## 222 How did the Priestly document get into the Pentateuch?

The priests of the Exile had the same fundamental purpose as had the prophets of the eighth and seventh centuries B.C. Both groups of religious leaders desired to make the people acceptable to Yahweh, that they might be recipients of Yahweh's blessing. While the prophets undertook to accomplish this by preaching morality and social justice, the priests attempted to do the same thing by exhorting the people to practice ritual holiness. They believed they could make them an acceptable people by regulating all of life, and by a multitude of ceremonies and laws keep them mindful of Yahweh. When, therefore, the great religious leaders of Ezra's generation—or perhaps slightly before—undertook to bring together a single book which might combine all the essentials of the Jewish faith, the Priestly Code was at hand, exactly what they needed. Likewise, there was the great book JED, and by combining the two they produced approximately what we have today in the Pentateuch.

## 223 Was the Book of the Law exactly like our Pentateuch?

In their major essentials the two books are the same, though editorial changes were made in later years which probably altered minor statements here and there.

## 224 Was the first Jewish Bible then an evolution?

There is a sense in which it can be said that the first great book of scripture of the Jews was the product of almost a thousand years of Hebrew experience with Yahweh. The best minds of the nation were involved inproducing it. The most devout souls of the race committed their most reverent thoughts to writing—the record of their glimpses of God.

## 225 What can we say about its inspiration?

The fact that it served to keep the faith of the people alive in the midst of their darkest days, that it inspired the most devout and lofty souls through all the centuries since, that it represents the best efforts of inspired authors to put the account of their inspirations into words, that it still has the power to inspire honest souls in search of divine truth, that it was born of the purest motives and most consecrated spirits—all this is evidence that it has come down to us by a devious and elaborate process through the grace of God and under the guidance and protection of the Holy Spirit. Let us read it, then, with hearts open to God, that through its pages, sometimes tortured and sometimes exalted, it may speak to us of the Almighty who "in the beginning created the heavens and the earth."